Her writings reflect a true love of people, a deep understanding of nature, and the beauty of a unique land. . . . Anyone who loves and respects the outdoors will enjoy this breath of fresh air.

Booklist
American Library Association

There are those who believe that the very existence of a pristine wilderness has a value to each of them regardless of whether or not they ever expect to be there. It is enough for them to know that there is such a place.

In Gunflint, *Justine Kerfoot has captured the essence of this enchanted place.*

Miles Lord, Retired Chief Judge
Federal District Court

Justine writes from the perspective of one who knows and loves the Gunflint area for reasons other than its wilderness values. She introduces you to many of the people and the animals who live there, and she vividly describes both the beauty and sometimes harsh realities of the area.

Harriet Lykken
Wildlife Task Force, Sierra Club

Gunflint

REFLECTIONS ON · THE · TRAIL

by **Justine Kerfoot**

Illustrations by Nancy Hemstad

Pfeifer-Hamilton Publishers

Pfeifer-Hamilton Publishers
210 W Michigan
Duluth MN 55802 (218) 727-0500

GUNFLINT
Reflections on the Trail

Printed in the United States of America by Edwards Brothers Inc

10   9   8   7   6   5   4   3   2

Larry Fortner, Senior Editor
Aubrey Freesol, Project Director
Joy Morgan Dey, Book Designer

Library of Congress Cataloging in Publication Data
90–63043

ISBN: 1-57025-041-3

*To Bruce and Sue Kerfoot
and Charlotte Merrick,
who gave me untold help
in the final editing
of this book.*

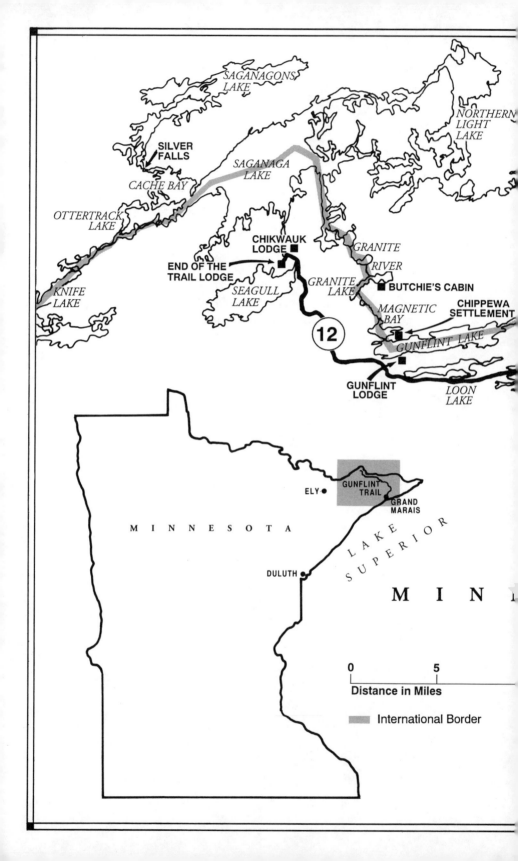

CONTENTS

Introduction

Epilogue   188

Introduction

THIS BOOK IS A COLLECTION of musings and reflections about life on the Gunflint Trail. Between 1958 and the present I recounted some of what I witnessed in my weekly *Cook County News-Herald* column. Some of the pieces in this book were gleaned from these columns. Other pieces were previously unpublished.

Many people have walked into my life on the Trail, and you'll encounter many names in this book. A few of my friends you'll see mentioned often. They deserve special introduction here.

Lillian Ahbutch Plummer and her cousin, Charlie Cook, lived with their full-blooded Chippewa mothers in a settlement on the Canadian side of Gunflint Lake. Ahbutch was affectionately called "Butchie" by all the local people. I knew her as a friend.

Tempest Powell Benson, whose mother also was a full-blooded Chippewa, lived on Saganaga Lake. Tempest trapped with her mother for many years and also guided for End of the Trail Lodge.

Irv Benson was originally from Duluth. After serving in the air force he guided for End of the Trail Lodge where he met Tempest.

Charlotte Merrick has been my neighbor and my friend for many years. More recently, in the past twenty years, she has been a frequent companion on my trips and adventures in the Northwoods and beyond.

The names of many resorts on the Trail have changed since I originally wrote about them. The Trail Center has become Poplar Lake Lodge. Balsam Grove has become Nor' Wester Lodge. The old Grand Marais Outfitters is now the senior citizens center. Saganaga Fishing Camp was later renamed End of the Trail Lodge. Sunset Lodge on Hungry Jack Lake is now called the Hungry Jack Outfitters. In cases where old columns, or parts of them, have been reprinted in this book, the original resort names have been retained.

For those of you who rely on calendars, the reflections and stories in this book are presented month by month. Otherwise, though, the material isn't arranged in chronological order. You'll move through the book from event to event, memory to memory, just as I have lived through the unfolding of time on the Trail.

Justine Kerfoot

Snowy Solitude

As I DRIVE ALONG, contemplating the intricacies of life, the car gives a gasless sigh. It is 15 degrees below zero, and it is midnight. I'll cover the last three miles the old-fashioned way, by placing one foot ahead of the other.

I am surrounded by a dark forest pierced only by the thin ribbon of white that is the Gunflint Trail. The world is soundless. In the distant north shafts of light appear, fade, move

1

and reappear. The clear sky is studded with stars that form clusters. With your imagination you can see in those clusters the figures that have acquired mythical names. This is not one of those dark, bottomless-pit nights; a dim starlight luminosity prevails. I think I can see the suggestion of faint shadows.

One foot ahead of the other.

What secrets this country holds. Once it was covered by great white pines whose canopy allowed only a trickling of light. The forest floor was clear of underbrush. Life patterns were different then. The creeks flowed stronger. The lakes teemed with fish, and migratory herds of caribou roamed the hills.

One foot ahead of the other.

Yonder hills once echoed with the songs of the Voyageurs as they plied the waterways in pursuit of the fur trade. Tragedies are revealed in the location of now-rusted flintlock guns placed on an ancient grave or the finding of artifacts where accidents had occurred in rapids. The portages have felt the tread of the roaming Chippewa, Sioux and Cree Indians as they struggled to maintain territory, or followed the animal herds for food. In later years, the portages were traveled by fur trappers and traders, prospectors, international survey crews, immigration and customs officers, loggers, firefighters, C.C.C. (Civilian Conservation Crews), forestry crews, game wardens and dog teams.

One foot ahead of the other.

Much of the country was swept stark and clear by fire and logging, and a new growth of tag alder, spruce, balsam, birch, aspen and jack pine took root.

This country was locally referred to as "back in the bush." The bush country was then penetrated by wagon roads and mining railroads with logging spurs. They were built by human crews with the aid of horses, dynamite and great perseverance.

One foot ahead of the other.

The gradual building of the Gunflint Trail, which followed in part the Indian trail from Gunflint Lake to Grand Marais, led to the installation of fire towers. These were joined by rustic fishing and hunting camps at the completion of each stretch of twisting, bumpy road.

Further changes came to the Gunflint Trail little by little. Communications evolved from an oft-patched "hoot and holler" telephone line to the current modern system. Gas and kerosene lamps were displaced by electric lights. Rustic fishing and hunting camps became comfortable modern resorts. Once-a-year snowplowing gave way to dependable prompt service on well-maintained roads, making way for a daily school bus. The gravel-corduroy road became a wide black-top. All of these changes, for good or bad, evolved year by year.

One foot ahead of the other.

The cold bites deep into my flesh where it should have been more adequately covered. Rounding the last curve, I see the welcome light that glows from my log cabin nestled among the trees.

Progress on the Trail, nestled deep in the Northwoods, moves slowly.

January, nestled deep in winter, moves slowly, too.

Our woodshed stands amidst a group of trees, protected from the wind, with 27 inches of snow on its roof like frosting piled high on a chocolate cake.

At some other cabins the wind has whipped the snow from the windward side and deposited it on the lee side of the roofs, where it is piled three feet deep. A shovel beckons, for roof beams can stand only so much stress.

Each fresh snowfall offers something new. Everything is clean and dazzling white, and it stays that way for weeks.

With the slightest breeze the loaded trees drop little chunks of their burden with a light thud.

In the late afternoon the sun casts a glow through the trees, making long shadows. A red sunset streaks the sky, which is full of elongated clouds that look like furrows in a field. A little later the full moon appears, hurrying ever higher and casting its beams on the gleaming snow, turning night into a subdued dawn.

The forest is full of activity—the trees seemingly shift in the moonlight and stretch to great heights. [1986]

A FASHION STATEMENT. There's at least one good thing about the Northwoods remaining cold for most of the winter: The current fashion is never in doubt.

Warmth is the key criterion rather than the styles that designers decree. Shall the waists be up or down; the skirt wide, tight, long or short; the hats high, flowered or cock-eyed? In the woods, fashion holds constant. With long johns, felt-lined boots, wool pants, parka, mitts and a cap with earflaps, everyone is dressed in the very latest.

The billowing clouds of summer that sailed and bobbed like masted schooners in a sea of blue, and the wispy mares' tails that galloped with abandon, have disappeared. Now the winter clouds are like the wrinkled brow of an aging man—unmoving and timeless as they lie somber and unyielding across the sky.

The soft sounds of a gliding canoe and the dip of a paddle have been replaced by the squeak of a snowshoe on a hard trail, the muffled chug of a snowmobile or the swish of a skier gliding by.

SNOWMOBILE TALES. By 1961 snowmobiles were in common use on the Gunflint Trail. Couples and children whizzed along with ruddy cheeks, enjoying the tang of the clear, clean air. The snowmobile was the new vehicle of choice for travel to winter picnics and ice fishing.

Out on the road, it was as common in winter to see a snowmobile in a truck or station wagon or on a trailer as it was in summer to see a car pulling a boat or wearing a canoe like a hat.

In the early years of snowmobiles, travel by machine was similar in some ways to the old way of travel by dog teams. The engines were small, making progress slow but sure with maneuverable machines that could follow the winding dog team trails and portages.

This mechanized equipment did not have to be fed when not in use. On the other hand, with the dog teams you never had mechanical trouble and never had to walk home.

The era of the machine has robbed us of the excited lurching of the dogs on their chains as they bid to be included in the team of the day; the lusty pell-mell dash on the trail when the anchor rope is finally released; the wild excitement of chasing down the frozen lake at the sight of a distant deer; or the expectant look for a kind word after the day's work is finished.

Traveling across the lakes with snowmobiles sometimes becomes a duel between person and machine.

One Saturday two men from Two Harbors set out with their snowmobiles for a fishing trip six miles down Sea Gull Lake to the Alpine Lake portage. They stopped a short distance from the mouth of the river running from Alpine into Sea Gull. They climbed off their machine preparatory to drilling a fishing hole.

While hard at work, one man turned around to see the front of the machine slowly sinking. Both men raced to the Bombardier, grabbed the bumper of the drowning machine and attempted to pull it to safer ice. But their effort only accelerated the sinking of the machine. To keep from getting wet themselves, they let it go. It slid quietly into 20 feet of water.

The men made a sad and cold six-mile trek back to the Sea Gull landing. The next day they returned and were able to snag the machine with a grappling hook and pull it to the surface. Weak spots in the ice have a way of getting a person into a heap of trouble very quickly.

Another time, Tumsey and Mildred Johnson of Grand Marais, who have a cabin on Saganaga Lake, took a Sunday afternoon jaunt on their snowmobile to visit friends. On their return trip on the far side of the winter portage and close to shore, a slight and unintentional detour from the trail landed them in an iceless pit. Mildred gave a quick twist and rolled safely onto firm ice. Tumsey clung to the machine and tried to urge it to safety. The skis reached the edge of the ice and, as if they were the hooves of a desperate animal, pawed furiously. But the machine sank.

Mildred and Tumsey, wet and cold, hiked the two-and-a-half miles to Saganaga Marina. There the Denhams dried them out. With the help of Rolf Skrien the men returned and retrieved the soggy snowmobile.

To add insult to injury, the Johnson's car was benumbed by the cold and only groaned when the starter was engaged. It took a campstove and other heating devices under its nether regions to put the engine in a starting mood.

In our North Country such a journey can be termed a casual day's drive, with a reliance on the ever-present helpfulness of one person to another—a golden way that I hope is never lost in this little niche on the globe.

Sue Kerfoot once took a Polaris Playmate down on the ice for one of our guests and shut off the motor while awaiting the guest's arrival. A few moments later, on the first pull, Sue learned that the throttle had inadvertently accumulated ice and stuck wide open. With a surging leap—like a dog that lunges into the harness for its first run—the machine took off, riderless and capricious, skimming the surface of the ice. It ran in an ever-widening circle, headed for a distant point laden with rocks and overhanging trees.

Two would-be helpers in hot pursuit on a second snowmobile tried to intercept the runaway, with the riders having a vague thought of leaping from one galloping steed to another in wild flight.

Their theory was never applied, however, for the pursuing machine came to a churning halt in a slush pocket.

The runaway changed its course and swung down a bay, through the brush along the shore and onto a dock in front of a cabin. There it tried mightily to climb over a snow-laden wooden bench. The snowmobile, like the frantic leader of an entangled dog team, was still lurching to free itself when it was finally subdued.

Snowmobiles can be like that—ornery and independent. A broken belt or a dirty carburetor or a big slush pocket can put the rider back on snowshoes in a hurry.

Once while riding one of these recalcitrant machines, a friend and I crossed a creek and gave full throttle to climb the snowy hill beyond. By the time we reached the crest, water that had splashed from the slushy creek and onto the machine's controls had frozen and rendered the accelerator and steering gear unresponsive.

Like a wild mustang, willful and gathering speed with each stride, the vehicle careened wildly up the winding trail and through a blur of trees with its throttle cable frozen wide open. The machine screamed to the top of the hill. Below, a long drop bottomed out in an abrupt turn, and disaster loomed before us.

We leaned toward a hillock and urged the machine to one side. The front of the monster reared up and the back dug into the snow, and we came to a sudden halt. The wild ride was over.

Crossing any lake on a snowmobile is a risk. With sudden temperature changes, cracks appear from the expansion and contraction of the foot-thick ice. Water seeps up the cracks and into the overburden of snow, producing a potage of mush.

A lead is a break in the ice which reveals treacherous open water. Yesterday it extended across the lake like a windswept river. Today it has become a trap of wet, slushy, sticky, clinging snow and ice.

So it was that in whizzing over Magnetic Bay with Butchie following on her machine, I lost the windswept trail by a few feet and settled into one of those slush spots.

Butchie watched me with amusement for a few minutes as I pulled, pushed and gunned the machine. "Why do you do this?" she asked. She stalked off to get a large armful of balsam branches. We built a bridge from the machine to the hard part of the trail and, after driving ashore, spent the better part of an hour cleaning out and pounding the fast-forming ice to free the machine.

As we returned home in the early darkness, a cloud cover hid the rising moon. In the deepening darkness only our fast, bobbing snowmobile lights skimmed along the snowy surface. We hoped to avoid new slush spots. [1989]

Once a year the Cook County Snowmobile Club took the border route from Saganaga Lake to Ely and stopped en route at Dorothy Moulter's to have a bowl of freshly made hot soup from a steaming kettle over an open fire. Dorothy, a registered nurse, made this location her permanent home and is remembered for the hospitality, directions for lost travelers and first aid she offered to canoeists in the summer and to snowmobilers in the winter.

In 1964 the snowmobilers were under the able direction of

Ken Skoog and Clark Dailey. The day had dawned cloudy with a temperature of 25 degrees. Twenty-nine machines, mostly reds and yellows, making putt-putt noises, were lined up amidst a group of about forty people gaily talking and laughing.

We all got off to a good start, heading across the southern portion of Saganaga Lake. Swamp Lake portage was the first destination. This trail followed the border to Dorothy's cabin on Knife Lake. It was here that we stopped for a lunch break.

Twelve Ely machines and their riders joined the group from that direction to welcome the Grand Marais group. Milford Humphrey lined up the entire group for a portrait.

The rugged winter beauty of Ottertrack and Knife Lakes, the snowclad cliffs edged with a fringe of pines and lined by a smooth white carpet, made an unforgettable sight.

After lunch, the caravan proceeded south to the now famous Vera Lake slush hole. There, by helping one another, we were able to lift, pull and push all the machines to solid ice.

After passing Ensign and Moose Lakes, the group inadvertently split up. Those familiar with the territory took the less-known, but drier route straight to the Fernberg Road, only three miles away. The rest of the group, now without their Ely guides, followed the conventional route up and over the Wind Lake portage. There we formed a human chain and pulled the machines up the hills and on through a swamp to what was known as the Basswood slush hole. Basswood Lake and the four-mile portage to Fall Lake, with the lights of Winton in the distance, called us on.

At last all the riders had reached their destination in Ely and were transported to a hotel to change into dry clothes and enjoy dinner. We also discussed snowmobiling and settled many of the world's problems which seemed quite trivial at that point.

The group had enjoyed a rare opportunity to see some

beautiful country in the wintertime. No one had a major breakdown or serious difficulty. None will forget the trip or the camaraderie.

Because of the Boundary Waters Wilderness legislation and the new restrictions on motor use, the last snowmobile rendezvous took place at Dorothy Moulter's place on Knife Lake on December 30 and 31, 1983. As of January 1, 1984, the area was closed to snowmobile riders.

Consequently, the winter beauty of these gleaming lakes and snowclad cliffs was henceforth to remain essentially inaccessible and unseen.

NEW WAYS. With winter trails for cross-country skis, snowmobiles and snowshoes, we have new ways to travel, new adventures—and new jobs. A trapping trail that had become plugged with fallen trees needed clearing and became a challenge for the three of us—Charlie, Butchie and me.

Charlie rode his Ski-Doo with a small toboggan in tow that carried snowshoes, axes, gasoline and the inevitable tea pail. I rode a Polaris Playmate (which I had been told was good for children and old ladies, but in reality is a workhorse) with a backpack attached to the back of the seat. The pack contained a mini chainsaw, gas, food, tools and other tidbits. I towed a short toboggan behind me. That's where Butchie rode.

At times we snowshoed ahead in the deep snow to cut out windfalls and underbrush and then went back and moved up the machines. We became mighty bridge builders, crossing and recrossing streams, changing our style of architecture with each construction.

Butchie pointed out a marten track. Weasel, mink, marten and fisher all leave similar prints, with the difference in size and spacing being the keys to identification.

At one place an old beaver dam with a slit in the middle, caused by an otter, let the water flow down into a clear dancing stream. This crystal clear water beckoned to Butchie, and she announced that it was tea time. We gathered around a spirited fire, drying mitts and sipping hot tea.

Here and there that day we saw where a deer, followed by a wolf, had freshly crossed the trail. Once we spotted a moose track. The wolves kill deer, but then, so do people. The hunter screams that a bounty should be placed on wolves. If the wolf could sit in the judge's chair, he would thunder, "Place a bounty on the hunter, for he is shooting my food." If the deer were allowed to express their opinion, it would undoubtedly be, "Bounty them both."

As we traveled back along an old abandoned railroad bed we saw an icy waterfall that was held fast in a decorative frieze on the side of a cliff cut.

A little farther on we saw a cross that had been chiseled in a rock face. A "dynamite man" on a long-ago railroad crew had been killed there and was buried on the bank above.

It was twilight when we buzzed out onto Gunflint Lake. The temperature had dropped to 10 below zero. The white expanse of the lake was bordered on the northwest by the distant gray cliff protruding into the pink afterglow. [1969]

FISH TALES. Like farmers who want to get into the fields to plant grain and find themselves facing a sea of mud, Northwoods residents also complain about wet weather. One week, our conversation wandered to the slush pockets on the lakes. Everyone was wishing for colder weather so conditions would tighten up and the going would be good.

If one waits long enough in this country, that wish will always be granted.

One day, Charlie Cook, accompanied by our neighbors Al Graykowski, Gene Groth and Jerry Mark, went ice fishing at Cook Lake on the Canadian side of the border.

Charlie caught a big fish that he couldn't get through the

hole. The fish had been hooked on one side of its mouth. Each retrieve brought the fish in crossways to the opening. Al Graykowski tried his luck without success. Gene Groth tried and failed. Jerry Mark sauntered over with a stick. When the fish started to come in crossways, Jerry pushed the tail down. That momentarily straightened the fish and Jerry brought it up so fast that the fish shot out of the hole. It was a huge northern that would feed everyone.

A husband and wife came up to go ice fishing at Gunflint Lodge one winter.

The man liked to fish, and his wife didn't, but she agreed to go along. To make things more comfortable for her, he drilled a hole out on the lake, set up a tent to protect her from the wind, fixed a bobber and line and placed a comfortable stool inside for her to sit on. He went off away from the tent to a better fishing spot.

The wife sat in the tent on her stool, took out her knitting and sat clicking the needles. The bobber went down. She laid her work to one side and pulled up the line, on which there was a nice trout. She rebaited the hook and went back to knitting. In a short time her bobber disappeared again and a second time she laid down her work and pulled up another fish.

In the meantime her husband had caught nothing. She called to her husband to ask how many fish they would need for supper and if two would be enough. The answer was unprintable.

STORIES IN THE SNOW. For two days the temperature has been above freezing and the weather almost balmy. The weather invited snowshoeing through the woods.

Tracks showed me the meanderings of several deer that had nibbled on a cedar, stood under a canopy of pine boughs, jumped fearfully in long leaps, or walked stealthily around an exposed knoll or cliff. The deer and I were not alone, for a moose had walked a short distance down the trail and turned off into a thicket.

A squirrel track and a fox track met, but it was a one-way track for the squirrel.

Across one stretch a grouse left a track as light and delicate as a filigree.

Skiing along a level trail at a slow pace—my pace—leaves plenty of opportunity for seeing natural sights along the way.

On a recent outing I saw where a mole had walked along the edge of the trail dragging its tail, and then had found the neatest hole about the size of a thimble into which it had disappeared. Several snowshoe rabbit tracks wove through the tag alder brush. From a nearby bush hung an abandoned bird's nest. It was about the size of a doll's teacup and hung precariously by three strands. A fox had run to the top of a gravel pile to look over the surrounding territory, and a pine marten had left its tracks as it loped across a snow-covered grassy marsh.

I came upon an overlook and gazed down on the lake that lay between high hills formed long ago by a shift in the restless earth. At the far end of the lake patches of blue brightened the gray sky, serving as windows and letting in rays of sunlight that gently touched the white hilltops. In the opposite direction squalls of snow threatened and faded. Far away, skiers were gliding near the lake shore, looking like miniature exclamation points on the move.

Winter sports were introduced on the Trail at Gunflint Lodge in the late 1930s. The guests were people who came from as far away as New York and West Virginia to enjoy the rigors and challenges of the North Country.

There were people from Duluth and the Twin Cities, too. They came to enjoy dog sledding, take snowshoe treks, ski cross-country on the lakes and enjoy our good food and hospitality.

In this period the roads were plowed intermittently at best, and there were no headbolt heaters for cars, nor electricity or running water for people. Wood stoves were used for heat as well as cooking, gasoline lanterns for light and cold outside johns for bathrooms.

The transition to better accommodations was long and slow until the late 1970s, when modern conveniences and winterized cabins were finally available.

Times kept changing as more people became outdoors-oriented for recreation. Now several lodges on the Gunflint Trail remain open year around.

The resorts on Gunflint Lake have created and maintained 50 miles of groomed cross-country ski trails. Several resorts at mid-trail specialize in snowmobilers and have extensive trails through the beauty of the woods that extend all the way to Grand Marais.

Other resorts before the midway mark also cater to cross-country skiers with another 30 miles of groomed trails. One family specializes in Mongolian yurts and overnight camping. All of the family-owned resorts offer a special touch of hospitality and service. The Gunflint area has become a wintertime mecca.

January was once a time of cutting and storing ice from the lake, hauling wood by dog team and snowshoeing hard trails rather than shoveling them.

In the 1940s and '50s it seemed the cold spells of 30- and 40-below zero lasted for longer periods of time than they do now.

The transition from January into February is now scarcely discernible.

Instead of being a place where we simply struggle for survival, the Gunflint Trail has become a destination for winter sports. Roads are kept plowed. Trails designated for cross-country skiing, snowshoeing and snowmobiling are maintained.

Today the natural winter beauty of the Gunflint Trail we once enjoyed alone is shared with many others. Some of us, though, still go out once in awhile and travel the old, quiet way—placing one foot ahead of the other. [1969]

FEBRUARY

Cold and Elegant

THE TALL, DARK PINES, like figures in a black and white
etching, stand draped in capes of snow. They flank the
Gunflint Trail in elegant silence, their glistening frosty caps
tilted at stylish angles.

Interspersed among the pines are lacy birch that bow
gracefully. Fresh snow caught in their bare branches shines
in the sun and reflects the colors of the prism.

17

The limbs of the scraggly aspen are flung helter-skelter, like the unruly hair of young boys.

The ash trees still cling to clumps of dried leaves, which they wear like hats decorated with scattered brown and buff posies.

This land in deep winter is harsh and forbidding and yet at the same time beautiful and inviting.

MOOSE TALES. We see more moose along the Trail at this time of year than any other. They come to lick the salt that is spread on the road by maintenance crews. By this time the moose have shed their racks, and from a distance it is difficult to distinguish a bull from a cow.

The moose feed on bushes and moss that hangs from trees. Because moose have such long legs they have difficulty reaching the salt on the road. They overcome this handicap by kneeling. It's a funny sight that greets you when you come around a curve and see one or two of these big hulks kneeling in the middle of the road licking the salt. They sometimes rise awkwardly and slip a little before they can right themselves.

One time we saw a pair of yearling moose that had struggled up onto the freshly plowed Trail. As they attempted to trot, they slithered and skidded. Carefully one young bull jumped over the roadside snowbank only to find himself belly deep and suspended in snow, unable to reach the ground with his hooves. He struggled and half rolled to extricate himself from his predicament.

I never cease to wonder how an animal as large as the moose can take a few steps into the woods and blend so perfectly with its background as to seemingly vanish.

THE SUN'S TRAVELS. Dawn hides behind a southern cliff as if to prolong that moment of silence before the birds awaken and the squirrels begin chattering to proclaim the expanse of their territory. Through the day the dazzling sunlight marches ever forward until it reaches the opposite shore. Then by night, as if repelled, the sunlight fades, step by step—the cycle to be repeated day after day. [1982]

ON BUTCHIE'S TRAPLINE. Trapping shacks have always intrigued me. When Butchie wanted to set up her trapline, I agreed to accompany her as a companion and self-appointed photographer.

It's always a good idea to have someone along. Two people can get into trouble as easily as one, but two can get out of trouble with much greater ease.

Butchie proposed that we spend several days at her winter cabin on the Canadian side of the border. From that central point we would cut trails over long-abandoned portages to other lakes in preparation for a later trapping period.

So we loaded up—Butchie on her Ski-doo and I with my Playmate pulling a sled loaded with our worldly goods.

The cabin was located in a stand of jack pine well secluded behind a hump on a point extending into the lake. Here living was reduced to its simplest form. This winter haven was a peeled log cabin eight by ten feet. The ridgepole was six feet high, and the shelter boasted a wooden floor. This sumptuous palace had a lean-to roof built over the entrance to shelter additional firewood. A carpet of boughs at the door served as a mat and kept guests from tracking in snow.

The shack had lots of locations to hang and thoroughly dry soggy winter clothes. As we stretched out on our bunks one evening, I counted 90 nails that served as hangers along the ridgepole and at the top of the walls. We had used only a smattering of the nails. Hanging at various angles were socks, boots, boot liners, pants, jackets, mitts, caps, wash cloths, towels and a lamp. There was still room to maneuver in a cozy sort of way.

We chiseled a water hole through the lake ice to reach our

water supply. A nearby dead jack pine was felled, sawed into chunks and split to provide fuel for the airtight stove. Our comfort was thus assured.

One day when we were checking beaver houses on one part of Butchie's trapping grounds, we discovered that someone had come in by snowmobile from the American side of the border and completely trapped out all of the beaver from the houses in that vicinity. The situation was made clear when I walked over a rock ledge and discovered a great number of beaver castors that had been thrown aside when the beaver were skinned.

Beaver castors are about the size of a small child's fist and are the strong-smelling sex glands of the beaver. They are used as a scent in trapping and in the manufacture of perfumes. We gathered the castors from the ground, as they were still in good shape and had a potential value. Butchie, who depended on her fur harvest for her livelihood, kept muttering, "Too bad, eh?" [1969]

WOLVES. Life is like a row of upright dominoes. Tip one over, and that tips the next until an entire row is down. One form of life depends on another. Wolves feed on deer, beaver, partridge, rabbit and whatever tidbits they can scavenge. Beaver are dependent on aspen, but at times will take willow or birch. Ponds, created by beaver to maintain their preferred water levels, serve as nesting places for all types of ducks and other water birds.

The natural balance is upset by human manipulation. Beaver are trapped with no limits. Partridge hunting is extended several months regardless of their winter survival.

When there is an adequate number of deer, there will be wolves. When the deer become scarce, the wolves move elsewhere.

A few years ago the wolves, with the aid of hunters, had reduced the Trail's deer population to almost nothing, the exception being a handful of deer still surviving around Gunflint Lake. Resorters and homeowners on Gunflint Lake started feeding the few deer that came in during the winter. The herd grew and spread. Word got around among the animals.

In human parlance we call this quickfire communications medium the "moccasin telegraph." I don't know what the birds and animals call it, but when one deer discovers a feeding station, they all move in—which is what happened. Soon thereafter a pair of wolves discovered this fresh supply of venison and established themselves on the Canadian side of the lake. They came across the ice to snitch one of "our" deer now and then. The wolves raised a family, and now they take a greater toll.

Perhaps we are remiss to continue to entice the deer with a generous food supply. [1971]

PINE MARTEN. Fred and Jenny Dell live on Voyageurs Point at Poplar Lake. Fred looks after many of the private cabins on the Point. On one of his rounds he noticed a curtain askew in one of the buildings. That was odd, so he investigated.

When he opened the door, the inside looked as if it had been methodically vandalized. Fred checked outside but didn't find any human tracks, so he inspected the inside more carefully.

The inside screens were ripped from the windows. The curtains were ripped to shreds, everything on the tables was strewn over the floor and the cupboards were a shambles. The window sills were chewed and a hole was gnawed through the sliding door leading to the bedroom.

Eventually Fred found the culprit—a very dead and very frozen pine marten. It apparently had climbed down the fireplace chimney. The screen that surrounded the chimney top had rusted away, and the fireplace damper had been left open. When the marten found itself in the house it went berserk and frantically tried every possible escape route, all to no avail. It had a beautiful coat and had been perfectly preserved by the cold.

Fred called Bill Zickrick, the local game warden, to report his find. Bill informed Fred that he was subject to a $10,000 fine for having a pine marten in his possession, but perhaps the U.S. Forest Service could add it to its collection of stuffed animals. He asked if Fred would take it to forestry head-quarters. Bill would then sign a release. [1982]

Another pine marten once took up residence outside a nearby winter home. Although I was aware that martens climbed trees, the female that I watched appeared to have been crossed with a flying squirrel. She would climb to the top of a tree and run deftly out on a branch to see if the branch would hold. If the branch was too shaky the marten would make a hasty retreat. If the branch was strong enough the marten would spring it up and down and leap through the air for another tree. She traveled so fast through the treetops that the swaying branches were the only telltale sign of her location.

Whenever the marten appeared a squirrel started to scold. The blue jays flitted back and forth trying to heckle the marten, who paid no heed. When a raven flew overhead, the marten watched it carefully. I wonder if all of this illustrates the natural pecking order.

Pɪʟᴇᴀᴛᴇᴅ ᴡᴏᴏᴅᴘᴇᴄᴋᴇʀꜱ. A pair of pileated woodpeckers have staked out a claim along one section of the Trail. Each time I take a friend along the route, though, the birds remain invisible. When I am alone, they appear again.

I am reminded of one such bird that once built a nest high in an aspen tree behind one of our cabins. It was unusual for it to build that close to habitation. A guest drove to the lodge one day laden down with tripods, cameras, wide angle and telephoto lenses. We discussed the bird, and the guest became excited over the prospect of getting a picture. He went down near the specified tree, set up all his paraphernalia and sat down to wait. He waited and waited and waited. The bird wouldn't stick its head out of the hole even to look around. I took a chunk of wood and thumped the tree trunk, which produced no results.

After a couple of hours of waiting the man picked up his trappings and departed. A short time later as I walked from one cabin to another, the great bird came flapping close overhead and looked down as if to say, "Foiled you this time." [1980]

LOOKING AHEAD. On the Gunflint Trail we savor each season and look forward to the next. With the passing of the colder months of December, January and February our anticipation for the next season becomes acute. These thoughts are often smothered in fresh snow a foot deep.

With each day's lengthening daylight hours the sun softens the snow. Travel in the woods becomes more precarious. To avoid an unnecessary struggle, it is wise to travel on the early morning crust and stay put during the day. As February ends the deep cold of winter is behind us. March will bring new challenges.

MARCH

Northwoods Spring

Spirits are returning to the trail, bringing with them drums that rumble under the lake ice with an ever-changing cadence. The treetops sway as if caressed by the spirits' gentle hands.

As the cold of the night fades into the warmth of the day the spirits stomp across the ice. You can hear them. You can see their touch. They ruffle the fur of a wolf as she trots on the still-frozen lake, and they romp with an otter as he runs and slides. These spirits soar with the lone gull that circles and rides the wind looking for open water. If you doubt the spirits exist, stand beside an ice-bound lake—look and listen.

LIKE A BOXER. Spring is like a boxer who comes to the ring with a sleek young body cloaked in a splendid multicolored robe and who, when you least expect it, pounds a vicious blow to your gut.

We were enjoying spring a few days ago when snow started to fall. The mild temperatures turned the miniature flakes into iridescent ice that clung to everything it touched. Tall pines wore halos of diamonds. The birch and aspen glistened and bowed over the road in great arcs.

The weather knocked out our power lines—still not an unusual occurrence. Candles and lamps appeared in the windows and the crusted snow reflected soft March light. Cabins and yards looked as if they had been plucked from old Christmas cards.

In this taunting beauty a group of persistent electric company linemen sawed and chopped and wallowed through the snow from six in the morning until midnight for four days trying to revitalize the electric lines.

One unsung heroine was Loretta Simon, who staffed the telephone at the Arrowhead Electric Company to take complaints and to assure the people about the progress being made on repairs. After all, when you can't turn on a light, use a stove or toaster or the bathroom, the electric typewriter or computer, the vacuum, the refrigerator, the deep freeze, the electric blanket or the TV, and the electric blower on the furnace is not functioning, what else is there to do but complain about it?

On the other hand, had you been sitting in a trapping shack with a kerosene lamp or a candle, a pail of fresh water from the lake, a crackling wood-burning stove, with a biffy

just outside, there would have been no problem. As one old Indian, Billy Connors, once said to me, "Why you shovel snow? After while it melt."

WHICH WAX? A fortune is ready to be made! All you have to do is concoct a ski wax that will glide at 20 degrees, stay firm at 30 degrees and still grip at 40 degrees. As it is now, with every 10- to 15-degree change, a particular wax becomes useless and rewaxing has to be done on the trail. No-wax skis? Snow on them balls up, too, as the temperature rises.

For budding chemists this is a challenge. Maybe future skis will be equipped with computers so the bottom of the skis can maintain a constant temperature. [1980]

NEW LEISURE TIME. Years ago winter vacations up here were hurried weekend stops. Now families and groups have discovered that week-long or midweek visits are possible and more enjoyable.

With better roads, more leisure time and the comforts of modern rooms and cabins people can ski or snowshoe back in the woods, where there is protection from the wind and where silence blankets civilization's sounds. The music you hear is the tapping on a tree of a woodpecker, the far-off cry of a raven, the song of the chickadee, or the chatter of the pine siskins as they flit from treetop to treetop.

SPRING WITH CHARLIE AND BUTCHIE. Charlie and Butchie and I sat on a snow-covered bank and watched two beavers swim quietly in the open water at our feet.

The first beaver was reddish brown and had cut a large tag alder near shore and dragged it along the snowy path to the water's edge. As the brush was pulled like a half-submerged raft, a tinkling of tiny bells was left in its wake where the shore-ice crystals jostled one against the other. The beaver towed the food to a newly formed house and climbed onto the sticks. She was rotund and appeared to be heavy with young. She nipped off a bough and held it in her front paws as if she were about to play a flute. Methodically turning and moving the branch, she ate the bark. She put the yellow, glistening stem aside, now a clean bone to be weathered by the wind and sun.

The second beaver was large and black and was towing a small poplar log. He pulled the log onto a flat rock, where he sat and nibbled.

The two animals moved onto separate ledges facing the water with their backs against a rock face. So perfect was the blending of colors that had there been no movement, we could have passed close by without seeing them.

Over on a shelf of ice was an imprint of an otter with its usual run and glide. We were caught in a fragment of time and space when nature seemed to be in perfect balance. In a few days the beaver trapping season would be open, and this peaceful scene would be replaced by the sight of pelts drying on willow hoops and carcasses cast to whatever scavengers might appear.

On another day we traveled on a backwoods trail. In the open water at the base of a rapids, two otters appeared. While my friends built a fire for tea they suggested that I go nearer to the otter for a closer look. I snowshoed over the hard crusty snow to a nearby rock and sat and waited, for the otter had vanished. Almost under my feet was an ice hole that had been open but was now glazed over and crystal clear. It was quiet except for the dancing sunbeams that skipped along the crest of the fast-moving water.

Suddenly, almost under me it seemed, there was a scratching sound. I looked all around cautiously to locate the movement. More scratching was followed by a quiet yet resonant umph-umph-umph and then a furry streak slid under the clear ice of the frozen air hole. Preceded by a telltale ripple, the otter appeared at the edge of the ice and lifted its sleek brown body half clear of the water to eye my motionless form. Then the otter swam a short distance away, climbed up on the ice and completely ignored me. [1970]

BEAVERS. A few days ago Butchie and Charlie invited me to go with them to look at a couple of beaver traps. We followed a crooked trail originally made by dog teams speeding through the heavy forest. Where a tree had fallen the branches had been trimmed to leave an arch framed by greenery but allowing enough space for us to duck and scoot under. Methinks there is an artistic trait in my friends.

We crossed several beaver ponds. The water had backed up in a small draw, killing the spruce, which now stood denuded and forsaken. From time to time we left our snowmobiles and used snowshoes to trek off into the woods to check a trap. We traveled over hills, through valleys, across creeks and on top of what in summer must be sphagnum moss swamps. We passed through stands of birch, jack pine, cedar, spruce, and aspen. All of this was nestled behind a range of cliffs and high hills.

On a sunny bank cushioned with boughs we built a fire for tea and munched on Butchie's homemade bannock and slices of precooked beaver meat. As I sat with my companions I was aware that this was a way of life experienced by few people. [1970]

THE LONGEST MONTH. A moose stood on a spur road leading from the gravel pit to the Trail. She stood motionless, knee-deep in snow, as we drove by. I stopped and backed up to the side road. The cow hadn't moved. She stood watching me, as I stood watching her.

I thought she had survived the winter in excellent condition. I looked again more closely. Her sides were bulging. As if she read my thoughts, she deliberately turned to one side, revealing her telltale figure. It is always that last month before birth that is interminable. She faded into the brush with slow measured steps.

SERIOUS AILMENT. At about this time of year spring fever becomes a serious ailment. The nursery catalogs have started to arrive. The pictures are so convincing that I can easily visualize the yard, still boot-top deep in snow, aglow with colors. Of course, all the flowers are perennials that come up year after year with no further care.

Many years ago at about Easter time I had a yen to start a tulip bed in front of my cabin, where the sun and moisture would cause the bulbs to produce blooms that would far surpass those grown in Holland.

The bulbs were planted, grew vigorously and gave great promise of future development. Buried among the tight tulip leaves were developing buds, protected like a blanketed baby laced snuggly in a *tikanoggin* (an Indian cradle board).

This was also the time when the woods around Gunflint Lake abounded with deer. On a clear moonlit night when dark almost becomes light and the shadows play tag among the trees, a young deer discovered this lush patch of green. I awakened to the sound of a methodical crunch outside my window. The tulips were severed one by one, never to rise again.

Another time the seed catalogs—enticing works of art that arrive regularly—again overcame my better judgment, and I ordered a batch of gorgeous-to-be flowering plants. Of course they arrived too early, before the soil had warmed in these parts, but they were duly planted. Before they had an opportunity to get a good start, daisies, grasses and weeds of all kinds took over.

Now as I drop the colorful seed catalogs into a box destined for the recycling center, I gaze out over the graveyard

of past efforts. Here and there, protruding above the snow-covered landscape, is the tip of a sprig. Is it a catalog bush trying to struggle through the winter, or is it just a dead branch dropped from a nearby tree? [1985]

EXTRASENSORY PERCEPTION. Sue McDonnell from Hungry Jack Outfitters must have the power of ESP. A group of Trail residents who work in town often pool their car rides while making their daily trips. Sue normally rides with Luana Brandt from Nor'Wester Lodge; but one day a little over a year ago she decided to go on her own. That was the day that Luana tried to pass a car parked on a blind curve at Swamper Lake.

At the crucial moment of passing a truck came around the curve, with the result that Luana got a jolting sideswipe and a car that was totaled.

More recently Sue has been riding with Bob and Mary O'Connor; but one day last week she again decided to drive her own car to town. It was the morning that Bob and Mary skidded on a curve and hit a snowbank. The snowbank would normally act as a buffer, but at this time of year it was frozen. The car climbed the bank and did a neat flip. Fortunately, they were wearing seat belts and were not hurt. Thoughtfully, they propped up a note on the upside down car saying, "We're OK. Bob and Mary."

Seeing the results of such an accident causes one to crawl back into the car and fasten one's own seat belt. [1981]

SURE SIGNS. These past few days have sent temperatures soaring into the 50s. The nights are barely freezing. On the trails, twigs and stubble that had been below the snow line earlier in the season are starting to sprout like hazardous spikes. Bare spots are growing on the sunny side of beaver dams. Creeks are gurgling and slowly gaining momentum and will soon be rushing with gusto.

Among the local people traveling the back country, there is a persistent question: How much longer?

When the slush ice starts to go there is very little safe blue ice beneath. Everyone I have talked to plans to be off the ice in the next week or so.

APRIL

Capricious and Beguiling

APRIL IS LIKE A NYMPH, capricious and beguiling, skating across the lakes, arms at her back, swooping by and then sweeping away as our hopes for spring pursue her.

The April wind whips across the lake and moves the ice, creating a jumbled ridge next to the shore. This buildup of ice is accompanied by a thunderous crash that is scarcely distinguishable from the boom made by a far-off jet as it breaks the sound barrier. In the final crescendo a meandering hairline crack appears and then opens wide. Anyone naive enough to enter this inviting lead may find herself caught as the ice field sighs and the channel clamps shut with the fatal suddenness of a Venus flytrap.

Just as suddenly and unpredictably, the wind subsides and becomes gentle, warm and caressing. The nymph turns and twirls in intricate figures, scattering sunshine, dancing to a silent symphony.

The trees high on a ridge stand against the backdrop of a sky of deepest blue, accented by a puff of cloud as light as cotton that tiptoes along the treetops.

The nymph is leading us through the transition from skis and snowmobiles to canoes and boats, from leafless stemmed *kinnikinick* to bursting willows. This is April.

SUBTLE SOUNDS. In this season the woods are filled with a silence so complete that some people are uneasy here in this semi-wilderness. Yet, if they listen carefully, they can hear many sounds: the banging of a woodpecker as it works on a bug-infested tree; the murmur of a whiskey jack as it eyes a tidbit at the back door; the stream as it gurgles and sputters to life in its collapsing ice cave; the wind that swirls a column of snow as it hurries across the lake; and the grumbling of the ice as it expands and contracts.

Then there is the ever-present struggle for survival. Leave the shelter of your home, and you may find a deer that has been run down and killed by wolves. I found one once that had been carrying a set of twins—two tiny fawns, hairless but otherwise perfectly formed in every detail.

A partridge, with its crop packed full of tree buds on which it had been feeding, had fallen where it had been struck by a hawk.

Nature, if left to its own, balances populations of animals by its ability to make environmental adjustments. Humanity, on the other hand, seems to be carried away by producing an excess of progeny that may eventually deplete the earth.

MA BELL'S HELPERS. All it takes is the right person with experience, ingenuity and know-how to outwit the problems that arise in this Northland. A Bell Telephone "cat," while pulling a cable across Loon Lake, hit a weak spot, broke through the ice and sank in 30 feet of water. Equipment was brought in from Duluth, and various efforts to raise the machine were made, but to no avail. Local people watched with amusement. Finally Bell grew desperate and the locals were called in.

Carl Mort, a logger with a small crew from the Backlund Construction Company, hauled long, heavy timbers across the ice with a double-tracked snowmobile. A quadruped framework was erected on skids over the hole. Bill Whipkey, clad in deep-sea-diving gear, dropped through the hole into the icy water. He attached hoisting chains to the submerged beast.

With a powerful winch the Bell machine's six tons were lifted from the water to suddenly become nine tons dangling from the framework above the ice field. A drum holding cables and powered by a compressor was mounted on the back of a truck. The truck was snubbed by a heavy cable to the biggest tree in sight. The suspended "cat," considered a small piece of machinery in these parts, rode in a cage like a portly prince as it was pulled 30 feet at a time.

The operation of these units was in the capable hands of Art Anderson of Schroeder. After a session of watching the recovery operation I hiked up the road on my way out from Loon Lake Lodge. On the road I met a portly, neatly dressed Bell Telephone man from Duluth, complete with dangling camera and safety helmet. He remarked, "Do you think they will get it out?" My response was, "Why of course, no problem, the local fellows are on it." [1975]

CARL BRANDT—TRAPPING. Until quite recently Carl Brandt Sr. of Balsam Grove Lodge was still walking on Poplar Lake. The ice was two feet thick out on the lake with openings along the south shore. The main body of ice had risen and was still white from the few inches of additional snow that came down a week earlier. But the places near creeks and narrows where there was a current were not safe.

While trapping beaver—traveling on the ice and carrying a pole for testing—Carl followed his tracks of a previous day near the head of a small creek. As he strode along there was a whoosh, and he found himself submerged to the waist.

Because of the woolen pants and underwear that he was wearing the water didn't seem cold at first. But before he was able to pull himself out the water had seeped to the innermost recesses of his hide and, bejabbers, it was cold.

After crawling out he came to the conclusion that his wool pants had absorbed most of the water from the lake and weighed close to a ton. He stripped, wrung his clothes free of water, put them back on and took a fast but mighty cool hike home.

Before his dunking he had encountered an unusual sight.

A bear had come out of hibernation, and Carl followed its trail on fresh snow to a beaver house. The bear had torn the top of a beaver house apart, clear to the beaver's sitting room. The bear had traveled to another beaver house an eighth of a mile away and repeated the performance. Carl also saw that a wolf had methodically cleaned up the beaver carcasses from Carl's trapping successes.

With spring calling and ice rotting on the lakes, Carl decided that this was the end of this season's trapping. [1959]

SPRING FEVER. It was one of those warm, sunny April days when the yen to go canoeing becomes overpowering. Charlotte Merrick, Doris Krebsbach and I put in at a winding creek where the water filled the marsh from bank to bank. We were carried effortlessly at a fast pace around a bend and suddenly washed into an eddy of currents that held us bobbing as if on a sea. We were swept over old beaver dams with a giddy rush and past empty beaver houses.

Farther downstream the banks were honeycombed with octagonal ice chunks. There were times when we slid aside to allow a fast-moving ice floe, twisting and surging in the current, to pass us. We followed the floes, weaving back and forth and playing a game of tag and near misses. The sun poured down into our haven.

An occasional pair of mallard ducks, startled by our arrival, rose to fly off in lazy circles but soon returned as if they had been disturbed only by a sudden slapping wave. The stream widened. We were faced with a lake filled with a gray foreboding mass of ice which had enough strength to hold us precariously and enough guile to suddenly yawn open a toothy hole and engulf us in an icy bath. We paddled swiftly onto its bony back hoping for a crumbling breakthrough. It was like skidding onto a living being. It heaved a little, chuckled an echoing laugh and slid us back to the spot from which we had made our surge.

Unable to reach a shore, we chose an abandoned beaver house in the creek for our lunch site. Like a castle surrounded by a moat with a flooded marsh near by, the house protected all who sought shelter.

Numerous water-boatmen (aquatic hemipterous insects) were emerging from a grassy shelf to be suddenly propelled to the surface and to scoot irregularly on their delicately padded feet. Larvae of some sort with forked, hair-like tails jerked spastically among the submerged grasses. A brown butterfly came to ride our shoulders and fluttered delicately between our heads. A pair of mallards bobbed and weaved in their courting maneuvers. A pussy willow bush waved a welcome from across the creek as we sat on boat cushions, munched sandwiches and drank coffee from a thermos jug.

From time to time a large chunk of ice broke away from the mother lode with a sigh and a tinkle. The tinkle was like the delicate sound of a far-off sheep bell on a mountainside. The sound was so distant and faint that it sounded almost ethereal.

The sun cast a long, waning shadow, and a silent chill settled on us. Paddling back against the current was a hard job. Our rhythmic strokes were accompanied by the overhead cry of a gull, who, unlike us, soared with effortless ease on the drafts. [1971]

NEW LIFE. Overhead a small, scraggly flock of geese works its way north with a weary effort. Underfoot, from nooks and crannies, new life slowly comes into being.

Snow remains on the northern slopes and in shaded areas of the spruce forests, but the warm April sun has penetrated and bared most of the land. After a winter of hibernation chipmunks are scurrying through the moist leaves. Crows have long since returned to herald the arrival of the spring birds. [1960]

MILKING WALLEYES. Those who have never observed the milking of walleyes as the fish make their spring spawning run would find it enlightening. Here at Gunflint the process is carried out yearly under the able direction and know-how of Jim Storland from the Minnesota Department of Natural Resources.

This year the job began while Cross River was still frozen over. A couple of DNR employees were sent up to prepare the work site. They made holes in the ice and then gathered poles, shoved them through the holes and drove them into the muddy bottom below. At the time of the walleye run cribs used as holding pens would be attached to these poles.

A few weeks later someone went up to inspect the work. No poles were evident. The workers had used aspen trees, a favorite food of the beaver who had severed the poles and dragged them to their underwater feed pile. The poles were replaced with jack pine posts by the DNR workers.

When the ice had left the lakes and the water had reached 47 degrees it was time for the walleye spawning run to start. A catwalk was constructed among the posts. A lead-in net was placed diagonally across the river to direct the walleyes into a catching pen.

The walleyes, ranging in size from a few pounds to eight and ten pounds, have been coming in at the rate of over a hundred each night. The walleyes have been accompanied by more than a ton and a half of suckers, which have been removed from the catch and will be sold to dog mushers for dog food.

A few small northerns have been among the spawners, too. It also was discovered that smelt are present in the lake.

In the critical part of the operation a ripe female and a male are taken to individual tubs of water. The fish are picked up one at a time, and, in a process called milking, the belly of the female is stroked, causing the eggs to eject into a container. The male is then taken and by the same process a squirt of sperm is added. When a little more than half of the eggs are extracted from a female, she is released to swim up stream and finish her job naturally.

When an accumulation of spawned fish gathers above the traps the lead-in net is lifted and the fish can then swim back into the lake.

During the milking the eggs are constantly swirled in a pan. A little muddy water is added to each batch of eggs to keep them from sticking together. A tub of eggs, with water renewed every half hour, is then taken to the French River Hatchery on the North Shore of Lake Superior. Some of the hatched fingerlings will be returned to the lake that made the egg contribution. The remainder will be distributed to other lakes in the state. [1977]

TWO PAINFUL LOSSES. Mary Netowance Plummer, who had resided for the past 70 years on the Ontario side of Gunflint Lake, died on May 16 at St. Joseph Hospital in Port Arthur, Ontario. Funeral services were held in Port Arthur on May 17, and interment was in Port Arthur. Mary Plummer, in her 80s, was the last of our area's "treaty Indians"—the Native people who received a modest stipend from the Canadian government.

She is survived by her daughter, Lillian Ahbutch Plummer; a son, George Plummer Jr.; and seven grandchildren. Mary Plummer was originally from the Indian reservation of Savanne on Lac des Mille Lacs Lake. As a child she and her family followed the caribou herds as they traveled south as far as Brule Lake. The family traveled on the Gunflint when the first blasting was done for the construction of the Port Arthur, Duluth and Western Railroad, which was started at Port Arthur and terminated at the Paulson mine.

Later, Mary Netowance married George Plummer, a trader who had a store at the narrows where Gunflint Lake joins Magnetic Bay. A hotel, store, customs and a coaling station occupied this site, which was once known as the town of Gunflint.

For many years, Mary Plummer trapped with her daughter, Lillian, and carried on the arts and crafts of lacing snowshoes, tanning moose and deer hides and making moccasins for winter use. She made birch-bark baskets for winnowing wild rice when it was gathered in the fall.

With the passing of these older Indians many of these arts have been lost. Mary Plummer was a lady one could be proud to have as a neighbor. [1956]

Mary Cook has passed away. Recently a local group of Gunflint residents gathered at the home of Lillian Plummer with the intention of moving Mary Cook, an ailing elderly Indian woman across the lake. She was placed on a toboggan.

Lillian, Eleanor Matsis and George Plummer pulled her. I have tried, without success, to keep up with George Plummer on other occasions and have come to the conclusion that he is made of spring steel. Mary Cook went sailing across the lake in speedy fashion.

Mary was taken to the hospital in Port Arthur. She was prepared for her overnight train trip to St. Boniface, where there is a Roman Catholic home dedicated to the care of elderly Indians.

These developments came too fast for this elderly woman, who could neither read nor write. She didn't speak English and understood only Chippewa. At the hospital she was stripped of her clothing. Her hair was cut short. The brusque but perhaps necessary moves infringed upon her privacy and created additional stress.

Although her son Charlie, with whom she had lived, accompanied her on the train to St. Boniface, he was not allowed to be with her in her compartment to talk to her and comfort her in their own language. She cried out for help and understanding all night. Upon arrival at the home she was whisked off to a room. Charlie was not allowed to see her or say goodbye. She lived scarcely a week and was buried in a potter's field. [1957]

THE FIRST FLUSH. Old-timers on the Trail may recall Dr. Remple and his family, who spent several summers in the 1930s at their cabin on Poplar Lake on the Gunflint Trail. At this same location they built the Northwoods Lodge, which they operated from 1936 to 1950. Mrs. Remple spent several years in Grand Marais with the children while they attended school. We didn't have a school bus then.

The Remples were from Estonia and had been swept up in the chaos of the Bolshevik revolution. Dr. Remple had been conscripted into the Russian army as a medical officer. Six-and-a-half years of flight from the Russian revolution and the

43

horrors of war involved travel by boxcar, wagon, train and on foot, living in and out of refugee camps.

Isaac Enns, a member of the Mennonite church in Butterfield, Minnesota, read about the plight of this group of Estonian refugees in a newspaper article. Mr. Enns offered assistance to the family to settle in Minnesota. In 1922 Dr. Remple and his family settled in Butterfield. Later they made Grand Marais and the Gunflint Trail their home.

Dr. Remple became the doctor at several of the Civilian Conservation Corps camps in the mid-Trail area. During his service he collected assorted lengths and sizes of water pipes that were dumped by the camps after their installations were complete. By connecting these pipes, which sometimes went from three-quarter-inch to one-inch to half-inch and back to three-quarter-inch again, Dr. Remple installed in his lodge a flush toilet. He then advertised that he had the only lodge on the Trail with modern facilities. This was the beginning of the gradual modernization of all resorts on the Gunflint.

AN UNCRAFTY CUT. Last year Dr. Charles Bagley of Duluth spent several weekends at Chik-Wauk Lodge. Although he had a heavy canoe of his own, Dr. Bagley used a lightweight canoe that belonged to Ralph and Bea Griffis.

Dr. Bagley later purchased this canoe, which was duly delivered by Bea Griffis to the Bagley home in Duluth. Dr. Charles moved it near some bushes and chained it to a tree.

Some time later he had an opportunity to sell his old, heavy canoe. In the exchange he was able to purchase a gasoline powered mini-saw. The saw was both powerful and easy to handle. While attempting to trim the tree with the new canoe still tethered to it Dr. Charles not only zipped off some tree limbs but, as the saw cut so easily and swiftly, he also inadvertently cut off parts of the canoe. The damaged craft was brought back and patched in Grand Marais. Ralph suggested to Dr. Charles that he restrict himself from that

time forward to surgery on the human anatomy rather than on a canoe. [1970]

Spring Fire. Sunday was a windy day. When a particularly hard gust swept by, the electricity went off, which meant a tree was over the line somewhere. Herb White looked out of the window and saw a curl of smoke between Road and Squint Lakes. He called the U.S. Forest Service in town and then called Gay Lynne Liebertz at Trail Center, a store and restaurant.

Last year the Liebertzes purchased a fire pump and five lengths of hose. Their foresight in having the pump, and especially having it fueled up and ready to go, no doubt spared us what could have been a bad situation.

Gay Lynne immediately called Jack McDonnell, Carl Brandt, the Adventurous Christians, Helmer Olgren of Clearwater and Gene Doody of Birch Lake. This group convened quickly at Trail Center, where the fire cache is located.

Beyond Bob Gapen's cabin at the east end of Road Lake a tree had fallen across the power line and had caught fire. There was an abundance of swampy water for the replenishing of the backpack hand pumps (known locally as piss pumps), which kept the resulting ground fires from spreading.

The fire was contained and under control by the time the Forest Service arrived. The purpose of individuals having pumps and hose has been primarily to hold back or curtail a fire until the Forest Service firefighters—who often have a long distance to travel—could arrive with more adequate equipment. This combination of resources has proven its worth.

Not that all are impressed. As Gene Doody was picking up a length of hose after putting out the fire a weasel suddenly popped up at his feet to protest the audacity of this trespass. [1977]

URGENT MATTERS. The birds have moved up the Trail in flocks. They flit in and out of the woods in their urgency to stake out a nesting claim before a competitor beats them to their chosen spot.

I watched a pileated woodpecker pound and tear bark from a tree. The bird stopped its feeding on hearing a mating cry from afar and hastily abandoned his meal to fly off for a tryst.

Squirrels pursue each other with the ecstasy of spring. I saw two chase each other back and forth until one popped into a small hole in a tree. The pursuer chased his lady to her spot of seclusion, but there wasn't room for two. He could only get his head and shoulders into the tiny opening. He ran up and down the tree in frustration and scolded and jawed. He sat on a limb, swinging his tail around in stiff angry circles. As he left in disgust the female coyly peeked out of the hole in which she was hiding. She silently scampered to the topmost branch and then emitted a saucy chatter. There was a scurry of leaves, and the chase started anew.

You never know how Nature will choreograph April's dance.

MAY

Season of Waiting

WITH THE COMING OF MAY, I am filled with the same drive that sends birds on the wing from south to north. I am afflicted with the same impatience year after year. But being an earthbound human, I can only endure restlessly as the earth and its other creatures begin to demonstrate signs of germinating new life and entering a new cycle of growth and regeneration.

I suffer doubly as winter, one last time, pulls the cord that releases several inches of snow, and our seeds fail to germinate and our plants shiver and regress.

April is gone, but spring is not here. May is a time of waiting.

ENCOURAGING SIGNS. Around the estuaries where creeks and rivers pour into the lakes the waterfowl first appear.

There are blackducks with their red feet. The green head of the male mallard appears with a satiny sheen. The hooded mergansers return, she with her crest and he with a dark head splashed with an arc of white that becomes wide or narrow depending on his courtship antics. Flocks of redwing blackbirds rise, circle and return to the swamp from whence they came. A kingfisher perches on a branch overlooking the water, ready to make a quick dive. A greater yellowlegs sandpiper bobs its tail with each step.

Rivulets gather and pour into a gushing stream filled with turmoil. The swift current washes the feet of small protruding cedars and sets a tethered tree to shaking with the frenzy of a Spanish dancer.

A gap in a beaver dam releases water from a pond with such a torrent that a small portion of the nearby road is washed away. The scene is watched over by four beavers. Perhaps when the pond is sufficiently flushed, or some appropriate water level known only to the beavers is reached, the animals will deftly plug the hole.

Inch-long catkins hang from the aspen trees while small green leaves dot the limbs. Patches of these trees, grouped on the hills among the darker green of the spruce and balsam, look like soft green canopies staked out here and there at a bazaar.

The stands of birch display unadorned twigs. From the right distance the scraggly twigs can look like an unkempt man's three-day growth of beard.

The north wind still has a chill. A smattering of snow lies in the swamps.

In a sunny glade the soil gives birth to a sprout seeking light. The woods are starting to burst into a verdant green. Yellow marsh marigolds line the creeks and azure violets appear along a gravelly road edge in the bright sunlight or peek furtively from the shade of a tall pine.

Along a marsh the bullfrogs conduct their symphony in sonorous tones. A kingfisher sweeps from low branches intent either on food or a courting mission. The mirrored surface of a pond is disturbed by the ripple of a beaver that glides silently across the surface.

Tiny leaves are emerging on the trees—some corrugated, some smooth and some still wrapped in buds. An ancient dead tree, collapsed from an old burn, becomes a host for ferns and moss. A large sawed stump marks another era.

A pair of mallards have taken up residence close by. The hen pokes among the fallen leaves and rocks. Her male attendant, at a respectful distance, follows a few paces behind. He is wary, always on guard, looking and walking with measured step. He acts like a suitor who has just eloped with the favorite daughter of a disapproving father.

The deer have started to sprout their antlers. Dark stubs three or four inches long adorn the heads of the bucks. The does are gradually vanishing as they drift back into the woods, from here to maternity.

A pair of woodchucks sit side by side. One reaches over, puts its arm around the other and then tips its head and peers into the other's eyes as if about to plant a kiss. [1974]

At day's end the sun turns the horizon crimson. Waters become still and wear a seamless reflection of the long, sweeping design of the shadowed pine.

In the dusk the deer nibble along the edge of the Trail. A shaggy moose ambles across the road, having neither shed its winter coat nor acquired the sleekness of summer. The drumming partridge repeat their wing beat in their ever-increasing cadence. This is our spring. [1969]

The long sun rays of afternoon sift through the dense forest. As though in an open amphitheater, groups of white and faintly-tinged pink hepatica are focused in a beam of light. They appear ready to pirouette and swirl, but alas, they are earthbound.

Constant subtle changes take place as dormant plants surge with renewed vigor. Ferns, still tightly curled, stand as if in reverent supplication. They later will thrust out their arms that are decorated on the underside with spores. In ancient times it was believed that the spores would make one invisible. Now I can understand why after spending time in the woods I can return and no one can see me.

This is the last magic hour of spring without mosquitoes or blackflies. In a single day or a single hour these pests will suddenly appear like an army in ambush to live out their individual life cycles with a jab here and a jab there. [1969]

WANDERING NANNY. Recently a fellow bought the Earl West mink ranch near Hovland. A nanny goat and kid were included with the household goods. At first the unhappy goat was confined to an enclosure. Then she was given some freedom by being collared and chained to a toggle. A big buck deer furtively watched this new being.

A few days later the goat seemed to be completely acclimated and was released from its tether. It was but moments before the buck appeared and rushed to the goat as if about to attack, but instead they looked at each other and sped off to the woods together—a buck, a nanny and a kid.

The new owner figured he walked 80 miles hunting for the white goats which were invisible against the white snow. The newly formed family remained elusive.

About a week later the owner glanced up from a cup of coffee to notice the nanny, her kid and the buck in the goat house. The nanny looked like a gal who had spent the night on the town, dragging home with her hair disheveled and hat askew while recovering from a beaut of a hangover. She returned humbly, hoping to convince her sponsors that her wandering ways were at an end.

Her kid was hungry, her udder was caked and frozen from dragging across the crusted snow, and food and shelter were more available in her own home than out in the woods. The nanny was welcomed and forgiven. The buck was kicked out. [1973]

WORK TO DO. Although conditions change rapidly in the spring, the general feeling among the resort operators is that ice will go out about the seventh or eighth of May. Over the years the usual time is between the first and fifteenth of May on the larger lakes and a week to ten days earlier on the smaller lakes. Predictions at best are unreliable. One key indicator we look for is the presence of walleyes spawning in their favorite creeks.

Resorters scurry all over their places in preparation for the spring opening. Late April and early May is the interim period between the winter skiers and snowmobilers, and the summer fishermen and canoeists. There is a surge of washing cabin walls and windows, shaking rugs and swinging mops.

The period just before breakup is one of frustration and restlessness. The winter is over but spring has not quite arrived.

A million things need to be accomplished before the first fisherman barges through the doors. We are limited in what we can do, because it is freezing one day and warm the next. Then, kerplunk—it all must be done at once.

We wish we had more hands, more hours in the day, or just more days.

As each resort opens its cabins and turns on the water, lo and behold, there is a split pipe here and a burst valve there. In the case of one new cabin under construction some of the plumbing parts had not arrived. The cabin was scheduled to be rented in a couple of days.

High water, frozen pumps or a pipeline through an icy area all present problems. Then after everything is working, a cold night comes along, pipes refreeze, and the process starts again.

TRAPPED. Peggy Heston of Heston's Lodge on Gunflint Lake has been bothered with a mother bear and three suckling cubs that took up residence in her back yard. The Minnesota Department of Natural Resources set up two live traps in hopes the mother might get into one and the cubs into another. They could then be transported to a new area.

When the mother bear was caught, the DNR was notified. Rick Fields was sent up to load the bear into his truck and, if possible, to catch at least one cub so the bear would stay put in its new location and not return.

Fields found that the three tiny cubs had scampered to the top of the tallest pine. They were crying for instructions from their mother, but no response was forthcoming. Finally one cub came down the tree.

Rick, who was well hidden, made a lunge for the little fellow. He grabbed a leg but it slipped from his grasp. The cub went up a tall cedar while Rick climbed after it. The cub clung to a limb and couldn't be dislodged, so a helper handed up a saw, and Fields cut the limb. As the limb lopped over, the cub jumped to an adjoining tree and started down. Rick hurried down his tree in order to arrive at the ground at the same time. In his hurry he stepped on a rotten branch, lost his grip and tumbled 30 feet to the ground.

Sharlene Gecas, a member of the Gunflint Trail Rescue Squad, was on hand. Mike Lande of Sea Gull, also a squad

member, was called in as a backup, and the ambulance was hailed. In the meantime Sharlene had applied a leg splint and had moved Rick onto a backboard, to which he was securely strapped.

Fortunately, his fall didn't result in a serious injury. The drop resulted in a cracked rib, a chipped vertebra, a twisted knee and a multitude of bruising hurts.

The Rescue Squad training proved its worth, for Sharlene carried out the necessary procedures efficiently and had the proper equipment on hand. All teams are supplied with emergency equipment.

One cub sat on a low limb and watched the procedure. The mother bear was taken away to be disposed of, and the cubs disappeared that night. It is quite doubtful that they would survive. [1981]

Early one morning two women were sleeping in a large home on the Trail. The home had a fireplace. Each woman heard from her room what sounded like a far-off thunder rumble, but the sky was clear. Someone seemed to be pounding on the door. An investigation revealed no one. The women sat on the couch pondering the occasional sound.

It recurred—a soft, thunderous drumming. It came from the chimney. The women realized that a bird, possibly hunting for a nest site, had gone down the chimney, triggered the open draft to a closed position and become trapped.

Opening the trap slowly, the women first found a webbed foot and then a soot-and-ash-covered body. The women grabbed the form, took it out the door and dusted it off until they revealed a blue teal, very much alive.

Upon release it soared and flew away, leaving a trail of ashes in its wake. [1982]

A DOE AT THE DOOR. She was pregnant and emaciated and stood at the back door waiting for a handout. As her belly jerked from side to side, the doe's discomfort was obvious. The tiny hooves astir within showed through the soft hide. It was foaling time, and a birth was imminent.

Days later she returned slender, wary and nervous. Somewhere not far away, a fawn lay hidden in the forest. [1974]

FACE TO FACE.   A short time ago I took a mask and snorkel and lay on a riverbank with my head in the water. (Brother, was it cold!)

Effortlessly riding in the back eddy were large numbers of walleyes, who looked into my face with appraising eyes. In small groups they would stare, then swirl off to one side to be replaced by two or three others.

Swimming beside them, like pilot fish around a shark, were almost equal numbers of red-horse suckers. They were large, sleek and more sluggish in their movements.

As I watched the walleyes from the bank, I noticed one big one that had made a run through fast water and was resting in the lee of the rapids next to shore. I broke off a twig and held it over the length of the fish. Later I measured the stick. It was 31 inches long. [1960]

TIME TRAVELING.   I have often been asked how long I have lived at Gunflint Lake. As of 1990 the answer was 63 years. Then I am asked if I wouldn't like to have it as it used to be here, with no electricity, no running water, an iffy telephone and rocky roads. It is an interesting question to ponder.

Would we like to revert to the period when dehydrated foods were unknown and we lugged canned goods over the portages? We buried the empty cans or sank them in the lake, as the U.S. Forest Service advocated at that time.

Would we like to go back to the use of canvas-covered canoes that became heavier with each rain storm as the summer progressed, or resume the yearly task of steaming and replacing a few ribs and recanvasing canoes each spring?

(I still shudder when fully laden aluminum canoes are paddled full steam ahead onto a rocky shore, or when I see scrapes revealing that these canoes are sometimes dragged over a portage.)

Would we like to travel again the roads that followed the ups and downs of the terrain and developed bottomless frost holes in the spring?

Would we like to adjust again to the Boundary Waters Canoe Area expansion, when private homes and family-operated resorts, through the power of eminent domain, were ousted from parts of Sea Gull Lake? (At the same time, religious organizations were allowed to develop and expand their camps into year-round operations.)

In retrospect I wonder how we kept operating our resort in 1936. That was the year of the fires—when the Forest Lake fire, the Long Island fire, the Gunflint-North, South-Rose Lake fire, the Northern Light Lake fire and the Kawnipi fire were all burning at once. It was before the advent of water bombers. It was the era of the C.C.C. camps, which brought in hundreds of boys to do forest management work. Luckily, this powerful force was also available to fight forest fires.

Eventually, when the C.C.C. program was discontinued and the camps dismantled, we learned the frustration of government waste. We were not allowed to buy any of the products that were left but watched as usable stoves, snowshoes and dishes were run over by a tractor and later burned.

Would we go back a step further to the time when forested areas were allowed to burn all summer unabated, when large-scale logging operations were carried on, and when a train chugged along the north side of Gunflint Lake to a mine site? Or back to when rails were laid and used from Cloquet to Cascade and on to Rose Lake in an extended logging operation?

It would be quite a decision as to which period we would want to exchange for the present.

WORK OF THE DEVIL. One early morning last week Archie Kirk Jr. called and suggested I drive up to Saganaga and have a look at the road. An overnight phenomenon had occurred in a swampy area a short distance beyond the Sea Island road entrance.

I found that a frost boil, or the working of the devil himself, had caused the road to sink into the nether regions, allowing a few hundred feet of road to drop into oblivion. Swampy water lapped contentedly in the new pit.

Ed Thoresen, a local contractor, was alerted, and at his call, truck after truck buzzed down the road. The trucks were loaded with gravel, which was dumped into the gaping hole. After the last truck had made its deposit, the road was reestablished.

The road had started to sink a few inches at a time a few days before the opening of fishing season and then sank farther. The trucks hauled and poured into the hole 3,000 yards of fill a day at a cost of about $15,000.

It has been suggested by Russell Blankenburg and other folks living in the area, that the road be shifted a few hundred feet to go through a rock cut and avoid the well-known trouble spot. Too expensive, they were told, for it would have cost $4,000 to blast through the rock. [1978]

WAITING FOR ICE TO GO. The weather! This week it has consistently ranged around 75 degrees in the middle of the day (even higher at times).

The snow has simply vanished, with only little blops left in the more shaded spots. The rivers are running over their banks in places and rushing at full speed.

By this time next week the ice will undoubtedly be out of most lakes. At present it is out of most beaver ponds. Iron Lake and Sea Gull River are now open, and a little wind will polish off Tuscarora, Poplar and other lakes of similar size.

George Plummer walked across Gunflint Lake just a week

ago. He said this was his last trip, as the ice was squeaking in the middle. I always figure Gunflint is out 10 days after George quits walking. [1957]

Searching for ice-out is like going on a treasure hunt. We have searched for clues in the highest hills, in the valleys, alongside streams, under cabins, near the lake shore and on a sunny hillside. Now and then we have found a clue that has led us on hopefully. It is the elusive spring we are searching for.

The ice is all blue, and bets for its leaving the lakes vary from the tenth of May (a long shot now) to the twenty-first. Even the shallow lakes are intact. At the opening of walleye season it may be more appropriate to rent ice chisels than boats. Walt Bunn has measured the new snowfall, which has accumulated to 11 inches. [1966]

On the Lake Superior shore gulls rise in a swirl like down tossed in the wind. Working under the constant circling and calling and swooping of these gulls is a natural part of every fisherman's life. The flurry of the wings is music to his ears.

On the inland waters the gulls arrive in pairs and with graceful glides ride the updrafts around open water. Their white bodies are a contrast to the dark hills, and their raucous calls bring an announcement of spring. On these island-studded waters the gulls come to build a nest, lay their eggs and hatch their young.

George Plummer took a fast ride down Gunflint Lake by snowmobile on Sunday. The tracks and glide marks of an otter intermingled with the human trails. Machine tracks and animal prints were built in relief on the ice surface, only to be obliterated by the sun later, in turn revealing the other layers of wanderings, like flipping consecutive pages from a notebook. [1972]

Irv Benson has made his final snowmobile run down Saganaga Lake. In places the ice was two feet thick and in others two inches. He buzzed around open holes. With each new mile his skin developed more goose pimples, for the trip was tempting the devil himself.

A couple of beaver trappers returned after camping three weeks in the Little Saganaga Lake area. They traveled on the early morning crust from pre-dawn until eight, when the stiff surface suddenly melted into mush.

Now that period has passed, and all the ice is mush.

The last time it happened was about 1950 or maybe 1951. The ice hung in the lakes that year until a breath before Decoration Day weekend.

Maybe the odds will be better this year, but there is still a heap of ice to leave the lakes. At this point the small beaver ponds still cling jealously to their covering. Snow is still piled along the shaded areas. Roads that were not plowed during the winter are still not driveable.

Minnie Staples and June Barnes of Poplar Lake just returned from their sojourn in Florida. They had followed the descriptions of our stubborn spring in the Trail column written weekly in the *Cook County News-Herald.* They felt we must be exaggerating the conditions. It was not until they stepped out of the car and into a snowbank hip high that the truth dawned. [1966]

OUR QUIET AWAKENING. Many of our summer guests have peculiar notions of how the ice leaves the lakes. To clear up misconceptions, I will explain. Briefly, it transpires something like this:

While still more than two feet thick, the ice is worn relentlessly by the sweeping, warm, spring winds. With the coming of the rains the ice turns black and deteriorates into dull,

clinging crystals. The ice is then termed "rotten ice," for it has limited ability to support weight.

Gradually the ice loosens from shore, creating long leads, and the ice cover is shifted by the wind from shore to shore. Crumpled ice piles up on land under inexorable pressure. It crushes docks, moves boulders and destroys anything in its way.

When a bay opens enough for the wind to get a real bite, and when the crystallization has completely permeated the winter ice, the water that is caught by the wind dances against the ice shelf and further loosens the crystals. Masses of the crystals become miniature icebergs that break off the main ice, slip into the water and vanish like raindrops hitting a puddle.

With a good wind the lake can be cleared in an hour. Without a wind the lake can remain dormant for a week. Ice-out is unpredictable and exciting.

As the ice breaks from the shore mallards return, and we watch with anticipation to see if some will waddle ashore to hunt for a handout. It is then we know that some who ate at our docks last year made their long round-trip flight to the south without mishap. They will nest near the cabins and one day will parade from their hidden spots with a fluffy brood of young ones.

The open water will soon bring pairs of loons to the lakes, too. On the Gunflint, as everywhere, spring is a time of stirring to new life. With the arrival of the loons our waiting will be over and our spring awakening complete.

JUNE

Life Unfolds

I HAVE LEARNED TO ACCEPT the pluses and minuses of June.

On the plus side, this is a time of regeneration. The woods are full of migrating birds, back from their winter sojourn, arriving to declare and protect their courting and nesting grounds.

Although I have not seen the birth of a baby deer or moose, I have seen little ones so young that they wobbled. In a few short days they are able to follow their mothers and obey the mother's grunts and other sounds.

In June the forest floor is covered with flowers. They too have their own niches—marigolds and Labrador tea in damp swamps, moccasin flowers among the jack pine, ferns uncurling to bask on the hills or where the sun has penetrated the protective canopy.

June has its minus side, too. This June is a month of frequent rains—not just light showers, but downpours often accompanied by gusty winds.

This is a time of mosquitoes, blackflies and no-see-ums. Before the development of new odorless oils and sprays, our main protection was a greasy salve introduced to us by the Indians. I always felt bear grease was its basic ingredient. I found Citronella was the next most effective deterrent. I went through the woods trailing this telltale odor, which alerted any wild creatures to my presence.

It seemed that after I had been chewed on long enough by various winged creatures, I became immune to their bites. I also always found it effective to stand beside an incoming guest whose fresh blood seemed to be more inviting than mine.

SPRING UNFOLDS. As spring unfolds to become summer an earthy potpourri of humus and decaying leaves is brewing up in the shady damp of the forest. Close at hand, rotting and disintegrating logs add their pungent, acid odor.

On rare occasion there appears a solitary or small group of fairy slipper orchids (*Calypso bulbosa*). Like marionettes on invisible strings controlled by unseen hands they slowly turn their faces toward the sun's light. They have a single leaf that rests on the ground and a stem of three inches. The narrow purple petals stand erect but overlap, protecting a slipper-like flower. The bloom is white mottled with purple and bearing a patch of yellowish hairs in front.

Canoeists hurry from one portage to another, while high overhead puffy little clouds lazily ride the thermal currents and laugh at the frustrations of the earth people.

Stand perfectly still beside a gurgling stream. What may appear to be just a glob of green slowly unfolds itself into an intricate pattern of fern or leaf. Close to the earth are delicate violets, white and blue, not much larger than snowflakes.

Wild strawberries have white blossoms that are visited and explored one at a time by a large bee that buries his head deep in the flower's folds. An anemone with a white face, centered by a tiny impudent green nose, is surrounded by stamens that look like suspended white freckles. Lacy ferns and others of a less complex design are scattered here and there.

Over yonder, close to the forest floor, are several trillium in full bloom. The delicate blossom hangs under a canopy of three large leaves. I must look from beneath to see the waxy flower with its three petals curled back. [1966]

IF IT LOOKS LIKE A DUCK. Largely through the efforts of Don Lobdell of Rockwood Lodge we are raising ducks. Mallard ducklings have been mailed to Don each year from Illinois. He then portions out the ducklings to various resorts to feed and raise until the ducklings are large enough to fend for themselves. Don's project has been a great success.

During the summer the ducks are tagged. As the ducks return each spring we can tell by the way they approach our resorts that they're "our ducks," not wild "outsiders." They come in fast with wheels down for perfect landings next to the beach and immediately seek out their favorite nesting site under one of the cabins. [1964]

This week the mallard hen at Gunflint Lodge hatched 16 of the downiest fluff balls you could imagine and promptly took them for a swim. As she proudly paddled by with the entire covey in tow, a camper from the public boat landing came barreling in with a net extended to scoop up the lot. I let out a beller like an infuriated moose and at least saved the brood from the immediate hazard. [1964]

In the summer of '65 Ralph Griffis gave a pair of mallards to guests who have an estate in Hamilton, Ohio. They took them home for pets for the winter.

Ralph received word one day that the hen had laid 61 eggs to date—some of which had been successfully incubated. Then came another call. The total was up to 101 eggs. Sixty-some of the ducklings had been hatched, and ducks were everywhere.

On the couple's next return trip they were going to box up all of the ducks and bring them back to Ralph. If you come upon a car quacking its way down the road, you will know the brood is coming home.

It is "a-borning" time again. The ducks that returned and cautiously hid their nests near the resorts where they had been fed in previous years are now displaying their broods of ducklings. Anywhere from five to a dozen babies trail after each mother.

Ducks feed heavily on the larvae and pupae of mosquitoes and serve a vital role in keeping mosquitoes in abatement.

The drakes have again taken up their bachelorhood until they acquire new feathers and are in demand to lead the flocks farther south. The males are flightless during August, when they undergo their molt and the acquiring of new feathers. [1970]

A TRAIL REPORT. Tucked like a tipped cup at the base of a half-rotted stump is an ovenbird nest with five small eggs. The location is near a cabin path, which seems to give the mother ovenbird some sense of security and little concern.

High overhead in a tall tree a blue jay has built her home, where the chicks will be rocked gently to and fro.

A large flock of cedar waxwings stopped during migration to feed in the pin cherry trees. In one tree a hummingbird hovered and fed for hours. Flocks of evening grosbeaks add a golden flash to the deep green of the pines.

This is when the morel mushrooms cover areas of the forest floor. Their spongy tops make delightful eating.

It wouldn't be possible to have a May or early June without a snowstorm, and so we were able to brew one up again this year. The snow covered the trees and the ground on most of the Trail.

High water is prevalent on all lakes. Portages are flooded in some areas. Several resorters are having difficulty getting to their cabins. [1965]

BEARS AND WALLEYES. We have pictures of bears on all kinds of signs: the entrance to the Gunflint Trail has one; the Forestry office has another; and then, of course, Smokey is on placards at every resort.

Along the North Shore there are live bears, large and small, penned up as tourist attractions.

Up in this country there are large black bears, curious and sometimes destructive.

Two families from the Twin Cities were en route to Chik-Wauk Lodge for a canoe trip and pulled in for a night of camping at the Bearskin campground. They carefully concealed all food, locked their car and crawled into their tent for the night.

At 3:30 in the morning a blare on the car horn awakened them. They scrambled out to investigate the commotion. A bear had pried off the left-hand door and window of the car and was contentedly munching on a candy bar forgotten in the front seat. [1965]

Walt Bunn has come to the conclusion that the appetite of walleyes is dependent on the phase of the moon. Apparently during the last full moon the fish were biting, and now there is a wane in the activity. There was a time that I could anticipate the activity of fish by watching other natural signs. I faithfully kept a complete chart of the moon, wind, temperature, barometer and thermocline. Each time a breakthrough seemed imminent, an equal number of exceptions blew up the theories. So, have fun, Walt!

THE SURGE. Have you ever watched a hive of honeybees? There is steady flight as workers flit from one spot to another.

This Memorial Day weekend delivered the year's first release of people en masse to their favorite vacation spots. Like bees they have buzzed in a steady stream into the North Country.

In town they lined up in long caravans in front of the all-night gas stations. Late into the night the procession plied the Gunflint Trail—fishermen and families, house trailers and travel trailers, U-Hauls and camping gear, car-top boats and canoes, trailers with launches, little boats and super cruisers. There was an array of truck campers, over-the-cab double-deckers, homemade vehicles large and small.

This scene repeats year after year as people seek a dream as elusive as the unpredictable Northern Lights. [1966]

As dawn sweeps into the sky, morning sounds fill the air.

At first it is the call of the loon repeated over and over like a signal for others to awaken. Ducks come forth to bathe, to splash and to preen. A bird calls from the treetop and is answered by another. A woodpecker bangs hard on a tree, and the echo resounds. And then, as if on signal, silence prevails. Daylight has come full, and now a new series of birds will declare themselves.

The surge of summer is upon us.

TRADER LEGACY. The Voyageurs who packed one, two or three of the standard 90-pound bundles of fur or trade goods left a legacy of French names for some of our lakes.

The Voyageurs worked their way up the Pigeon River at Lake Superior to South Fowl Lake, which was named at that time Lac Aux Outards (the Lake of the Canada Goose), then on through Moose Lake—where Mackenzie declared the whitefish exquisite.

Mountain Lake originally had the Chippewa name Keesh-ku-Lagayan, or the Lake of the Hills.

Rose Lake's Chippewa name is Ka-ba-Gouish-ke-wa-ga. Rose Lake was also known at one time as the Talking Cliffs —for your voice projected there will echo back to you five or six times. [1967]

STRIKE ONE. The world has tilted on its axis, and a monsoon period has descended upon us.

The rains have more than made up for the lack of snow that we had this winter.

In particular, the headwaters of the Hudson Bay flowage are most greatly affected. Our shores and cabin paths have become flooded.

Along with the summer deluge came a lightning and thunder storm. On Saganaga the Sandes were tucked snugly into bed when a bolt of lightning hit an aerial, followed it into their radio, jumped to the bedstead and killed their pet dog, Taffy, who was lying on a rug beside the bed. Mrs. Sande received a shock that momentarily paralyzed her arm. They came through the experience shaken and very sad about the dog, but otherwise unharmed.

At Sea Gull Lodge a transit had been erected and showed exactly a 12-inch rise in Sea Gull Lake.

At Gunflint Lake the water has completely inundated the dock area. I could paddle along the lower paths in front of the cabins. The water is still rising. There is no longer a rapids between Little Gunflint and Little North Lake, just a wide, fast-flowing river.

For at least a week after these headwaters start to go down, Saganaga will continue to rise until the water can be carried off by the one big outlet at Silver Falls. During this transition Ralph Griffis may send out an SOS for sandbags and people to create a dike to attempt to save his newly-constructed putting green. [1968]

ON THE SOUTH BRULE RIVER. A bull moose splashed along a marsh. He wore a great velvet ornament that extended some four feet on each side of his head with an overlap in front of his eyes like a military cap. The usual curved back-sweep ordinarily worn by bulls was missing.

The moose spotted me observing and, startled, hurried from the water to higher ground, stepped on some slippery boulders and fell forward onto his chin. With seeming embarrassment he rose, stalked to a cleared, level area and watched with dignified disgust as the intruder who had caused the mishap continued on her own way.

As I glided quietly in a canoe down the Brule River, blackducks ahead of me splashed and fed. I approached closer and the males flew away like cowards. A female swam toward shore with a brood of a half-dozen ducklings nestled close to her side. She slid under the overhanging brush and became completely invisible.

Around a curve a deer stood at the water's edge. Intent upon feeding, it neither heard nor saw the approaching canoe. I, now within 10 feet and trying to hold the canoe back, inadvertently splashed my paddle like a light beaver smack. The deer looked up with a start and leaped high in a graceful arc with water flying. Upon reaching the protection of a fringe of trees, it snorted and stamped in defiance.

Circular dew-laden spiderwebs sparkled with reflected light in the early morning sun. White bunchberry plants

spread through the woods, and purple bluebells clung to crevices along the rocks in the spray of waterfalls.

In the marshy pond near Chik-Wauk Lodge a bittern has called morning and evening. It took some sleuthing for Ralph Griffis to locate the source of what sounded like a "one-lung pump" just getting under way.

A week ago a mallard who nested on a cliff above the water had babies who had pipped their shells and later emerged. As Ralph watched the mother dropped off the cliff and into the water, followed by eight bits of floating down. They landed gently and paddled off with vigor.

A bear wandered around Heston's Lodge, showing no fear. It had a pal who decided to investigate a cabin belonging to Al Graykowski, a neighbor. Perhaps the cabin was just an obstacle in its line of travel, for the bear went in one window, across the cabin and out the opposite window. [1968]

EVE BLANKENBURG IS EXPECTING! A few days ago Russell Blankenburg stepped from his house to pick up a canoe to send out with a party on a canoe trip. As he leaned over a partridge ran around attacking his feet and raising a real ruckus.

Upon investigation Russell discovered a nest with 16 eggs under the canoe. He carefully removed the canoe and immediately replaced it with another.

Eve has been making frequent trips to see how soon she is going to be a grandmother. Eve will have to watch closely, for within an hour after hatching, the downy ones will be led away to be hidden in the woods under a cover of leaves and brush. [1969]

THE ART OF FLY FISHING. I finally conned Charlie Ott, a retired game warden, who, with John Aman, was working for me at the Grand Marais Outfitters, to take me brook trout fishing.

He was to instruct and demonstrate the art of fly casting along a bushy stream off the Gunflint Trail. I had a rod, line and reel, which he rigged with the proper leader and an attractive fly that he plucked from an overflowing box.

He furnished me with a pair of knee-high waders to keep my feet dry and three pairs of wool socks to help take up the roominess of the boots (my toes were still two inches from the end). Then Charlie led me to an enticing stream, where an occasional swirl indicated a trout was feeding.

Charlie instructed me to plop the fly out yonder and not fish in one spot but to work downstream. Then he eased upstream and disappeared around a corner.

I don't suppose this fly casting business could be too difficult, I thought. I had practiced on the front lawn at Gunflint and watched it demonstrated at sports shows. But now with a slight breeze, with brush around me and snags behind me, I was dealing with unanticipated handicaps. Occasionally I landed the fly midstream, but more often I deposited it in brush and snags.

I had heard somewhere that a snitch of worm on a hook, tossed into the current and allowed to coast downstream, produced more predictable results than fishing with a fly. That passing fancy had to remain deeply buried in my mind, for to mention such a thought to a fly fisherman was a complete sacrilege.

After a cast or two (or, to use the vernacular, after I laid the fly gently on the flowing water), I caught my first flopping trout. I let out a whoop, but it fell on deaf ears, for Charlie had long since departed far upstream.

My victory was short lived. I soon discovered that the fly line had an uncanny faculty for tangling in my boot laces. And, as I stepped into a hidden beaver run, I found my knee-high boots made exceptional water containers.

Finally Charlie wandered back with eight brookies, which assured a good meal for John, Charlie and me. Fly fishing is

challenging, and I can hardly wait until I have another chance to outsmart the buggers.

About a week later my instructions in flyfishing came to a halt. Charlie had taken me out on a small lake for a couple of hours to perfect my flycasting technique.

I was casting from the boat as we passed a narrow waterway between the main shore and an island. Charlie alerted me to watch out for an overhanging cedar, as he didn't want to climb a tree to retrieve a fly.

The words were still floating from his lips when the sailing fly—seemingly of its own volition—rose higher and higher and did a neat back loop around the topmost branch. Charlie wouldn't let me break the line. After all, his pet fly was on the end of it—so he climbed!

A little later in the day I landed the fly dead center in the back of his shirt. He couldn't reach it from the bottom or from the top. He could retrieve it only by removing his shirt.

Now I am on my own, but I understand that is the way brook trout fishermen are supposed to be. [1969]

Have you ever seen a fly tree? Your perusal of all the tree books will fail to reveal the species. The one that I discovered hangs willowy over a bubbling stream that leads to a quiet pool. The limbs drape in slender arches and end in broad, irregular leaves. As the sunlight sifts through its canopy you can see several bud-like protuberances clinging to the stems and glittering with specks of gold or flecks of red.

The tree is truly a mutation—a tree littered with my trout flies. Don Larmouth was the benefactor who had bestowed upon me these tiny bits of beauty that now adorn the fly tree. I bemoan my fate.

A girl with freckles and auburn hair strolled into the Grand Marais Outfitters in town. John Aman asked if he could have a lock of her hair. She obliged. John dashed down the street to the Beaver House bait shop and went into a huddle with Marti Cronberg, who ties flies and makes jigs. Within the hour I was presented with an enticing fly—reddish, delicate and dainty, but lacking the freckles.

Don Larmouth strolled by and just happened to have in a plastic jewel box two more gems to replace my losses. Charlie Ott presented me with one of his favorites, recently tied by Marti, that I could see would practically dance with fairy steps down a winding stream. I have a feeling that a concerted move is on to keep me from reverting to worms. It might be more practical to preserve these bits of delight and have them mounted as lapel pins.

WEE ONE. The loons call near their nesting places on most lakes. They have a brood of two or three babies that take turns riding snugly on the back of the mother. I once saw a baby being "warmed up" under a mother's wing. The baby had disappeared, and I feared it had been grabbed off by a northern pike, when suddenly the parent lifted its wing slightly, and out popped the wee one.

YES, WE CAN. Who wants to walk a mile with me? I have come to the conclusion that if each of us would walk one mile and pick up the cans along the road, we could make a big improvement.

It is easy to grouse and complain, but doing something constructive would not only improve the Trail but also help maintain a good waistline.

As a result of a Gunflint homeowners' meeting it was decided that a can pickup would be started on one portion of the Trail. Starting at the Loon Lake public access and working both ways, Gunflint homeowners will be dropped off at intervals of one mile. Each person will be furnished

with a garbage bag. The cans and bottles we'll pick up have been tossed from cars.

At the termination of this activity a sign should be placed at each end of the strip reading, "You are now entering a clean area created by the people who care." [1972]

The effort had its rewards, for now there is an all-out Trail cleanup. The pickup extended from the End of the Trail Lodge to the Trout Lake turnoff. There were 30 young people from the Plymouth Youth Camp on Sea Gull Lake working on the upper end of the Trail and 30 from Okontoe working the lower end of the Trail. In between were homeowners, resorters and a few foresters.

About 220 bags of cans and papers were filled, stacked and picked up. In addition to the bags, there were tires, mufflers, tailpipes, a bed spring, a garbage can, wheel rims and hub-caps.

As Eve Blankenburg and Pat O'Leary of the Forest Service were working one stretch, a car came along and someone flipped a can out of the window. Eve said if she had held the bag wide open, she thought she might have caught it. Her prize find was a full jug of Clorox.

This is the second year that this effort has been made to clean the Trail, and there seemed to be less debris than last year. With the present heavy traffic on the Trail, just think what a five-year accumulation would look like if it were all strung along the pavement.

Irene Baumann of Golden Eagle Lodge organized the groups on the lower end of the Trail and Eve Blankenburg of Sea Gull Lake organized the upper end. Gene Gasper, who headed the Gunflint Lake homeowners, did a great job in marking mile intervals for the group of 16 who turned out for their detail.

The job has many rewards: It shows we care about the looks of the Trail, it gives us some exercise and it could be a fun day. In a way it reminds me of when I started raising a family and had to wash diapers. I could hardly wait for the time when the youngsters were finally "trained." If we could only housebreak the public who are careless with their cans and debris, we would have it made! [1981]

FIRE WATCHERS. In the past fire lookout towers were scattered throughout the area on high hills within sight of each other. They were usually staffed by a single ranger, who scanned the horizon day after day for a wisp of smoke. I do not recall that they worked only eight hours a day, five days a week.

For the most part theirs was a lonely vigil. Anyone who came to visit and climb the straight-up, unguarded ladder to the little cupola that sat like a tree house perched on a toothpick was warmly welcomed and instructed in the art of spotting a fire.

Twice a week we took our guests at Gunflint Lodge to hike up the hill from the Gunflint Trail, climb the tower and visit the ranger.

Towers were located at strategic points such as Gunflint, Lima Mountain, West Bearskin, Pine Mountain and elsewhere throughout the county. Fire spotting was then only supported by airplanes.

Gradually, though, the planes took over the complete patrolling, and the towers were no longer staffed. They remained a nostalgic landmark of other days. Eventually they were sold and dismantled. Look no more to those hills for the familiar spires. [1973]

In 1945 Vic Sipka was one of the last tower watchers to work at the Gunflint lookout tower. Upon his retirement he acquired a home on Devil's Track Lake.

Last week, at about 6:30 in the evening, he was anchored on the lake, still-fishing for walleyes. He noticed a couple who came onto the lake from Bjchee's Lodge, where they were guests. They had their own boat, which was a duck boat 10 feet long and 32 inches deep with a 3-horse motor. The man weighed 210 pounds and was accompanied by a gal who was a slight 125 pounds.

They plowed along on the water with about three inches of freeboard. Vic watched them with idle curiosity as they disappeared behind an island. Suddenly he heard shouts for help. He pulled anchor and went to the rescue. This time it wasn't a forest fire but a dunking. The couple had swamped in about 35 feet of water.

The woman was swimming away from the boat and shouting for Vic to save her companion, as he couldn't swim a stroke. Vic first dragged her, already exhausted, into his boat and then towed the man ashore. They were not wearing life jackets, but each had a floating cushion.

After the rescue, as they lifted ashore their cooler containing a half bottle of gin—the only material thing to survive the overturn—they turned to Vic and said, "Sure glad you were around," and tramped off to their cabin.

You may draw your own conclusions from this incident. [1973]

STRIKE TWO. A family of five on a canoe trip from Tuscarora Outfitters was camping out on the shore of Saganagons Lake in the Quetico. They had two tents—a small one and a large four-person tent.

They watched an approaching storm and decided minutes before it was upon them to all go into the larger tent and have a game of cards. They had just assembled when a bolt of lightning hit a tree next to the small tent, shredding the bark all the way down. The lightning jumped to the zipper of the tent, then to the zippers on the sleeping bags, which were completely shredded. The bolt went through the tent floor and made a hole in the ground. It dissipated enough so that when it reached the adjoining tent just one person suffered from minor leg burns.

The tent that had been struck by the lightning was in shambles, with shredded bark inside and outside. [1975]

SEA GULL SPUR. Gunflint Trail originally ended at Gunflint Lake near the present public boat landing. Much of the Trail was made up of parts of an old Indian trail to what is now Grand Marais.

The trail to Gunflint Lake eventually became an auto road of sorts and was extended to Gunflint Lodge in about 1922. By 1930 a spur was extended from the Gunflint Trail to Sea Gull Lake and for a couple of years was referred to locally as the Sea Gull Road. A private road was then extended from Sea Gull to Saganaga Lake. It was built and maintained jointly by the Blankenburgs and Art Nunstead for several years to service their two resorts—Saganaga Fishing Camp, owned by the Blankenburgs, and Chik-Wauk Lodge owned by Art Nunstead. They charged a toll to anyone using the road other than their clientele.

Later they offered the road to Cook County, which accepted the offer and assumed responsibility for the road.

Even at the time of the original construction, another route might have been more desirable but could not be planned, for it would have crossed government forest land, which at that time was taboo. [1977]

CHARLOTTE POWELL'S PARTY. Some 60 people came to the party given in Charlotte Powell's honor by Bea and Ralph Griffis at Chik-Wauk Lodge to celebrate her 70th birthday. In reality it was just a moment's hesitation in Charlotte's busy daily schedule. She zips up the lake with the mail triweekly, cooks for groups of homeowners, and helps clean cabins when needed for End of the Trail and Chik-Wauk Lodges.

As someone said, she talks, walks and writes at the same

speed—which, believe me, is fast. Among the many gifts were three dozen bars of Three Musketeers, her favorite candy. [1970]

VANISHED. I drove the car onto a high hill in an area that had been logged and replanted. As I started to make a turn, my companion shouted, "Stop! Stop! Or you'll kill her."

Not knowing what my companion was referring to, I stopped. Before us was a killdeer with spread wings, about to take on and kill, if necessary, our car—this beast that was threatening her nest and its four unhatched eggs.

Normally, killdeer distract intruders from finding their nest by fluttering off with their injured-wing act. This one, however, stood by her nest, her beak extended and her wings and tail feathers spread as she challenged any newcomers.

A short distance away a pair of kingfisher had established a nest in a sandy-clay hole which was almost a quarter of a mile from the nearest pond. These ground nests are some-times located at the end of a five- to ten-foot tunnel. The young remain secluded for about four weeks. If undisturbed killdeer and kingfisher often return to the same area in subsequent years.

I often have gone to the promontory and perched on a pile of logs that had been left to rot from a logging operation. From there I can overlook a valley, denuded of its cover of spruce trees, and the timbered hills beyond.

The valley fills with grass that by the end of the summer is almost shoulder high. Moose and bear trails cross this stretch of the terrain.

From my position I have watched the killdeer tending her nest and her mate feeding nearby. I felt as if I had established a transitory rapport with this bird—an unexplained attach-ment. Each year I made the trip to see if they would return and, when they did, I felt glad to see them and wanted to acknowledge their presence.

There came a time when the authorities decided to spray the area, which would kill not only the existing birch and deciduous trees but also the underbrush, allowing the small trees that had been planted in the cutover area to survive without competition.

Late this spring, after the killdeer returned and laid her eggs, I noticed a lethargy in the female, and the male did the broken-wing act as if slightly drunk. I watched them during the summer, and their actions seemed to be growing more disoriented. I concluded that the spray that had been used to retard the undergrowth was slowly creating an increasing accumulation of poison in their bodies as they fed. The female let me walk up to the nest without stirring. When it was time for hatching, I went to have another look. There were no birds, no babies, no egg shells! It was as if they had been spirited away.

The killdeer vanished, leaving nary a trace, for they build no nest but lay their eggs on the ground in a slight depression. They never returned, and I felt sad at their passing. [1981]

BEN AMBROSE.   Ben Ambrose, now 85, is one of those people who turned over his land within the BWCA to the government with the stipulation that he could remain on the land for his lifetime. Ben lives on Ottertrack Lake. He has spent most of his life in the woods earning a living at trapping, guiding and prospecting. He also has a yen for flowers and a vegetable garden.

At his place on Ottertrack he has terraced a hillside and provides himself with fresh produce during the summer. For years he has bought plants from Howard Joynes, who started the plants in his own garden in Grand Marais.

This year Ben "came in" again and purchased tomato plants two feet tall and heavy with fruit along with other vegetable plants and flowers. Ben figured it would take four

trips across Monument Portage to get his bounty safely from Saganaga Lake to Ottertrack Lake. More power to him as he approaches his 86th birthday. He lives alone in a small cabin, where his needs are simple. [1981]

SIGHTS. The moose was submerged except for a black hump that resembled a rock protruding from the still waters of a beaver pond.

The head rose as the big jaws munched slowly on water lily roots. His large ears hung limp. The new growth of antlers in velvet was palmated and flat like a mitt without fingers. He shook his head and water sprayed in all directions. His ears became erect. He stood for a moment, looking and listening. His ears flopped back down, and he again submerged.

A high hill protected the pond on one side. A redwing blackbird called from the top of a stub. A duck silently glided along the edge of the marsh grass with her string of newborn following while exploring and making quick jabs at a bug or two.

The tourist who impatiently hurries from one place to another misses these sights. [1982]

ALONG THE ROAD. The evening grosbeaks have gathered in flocks on the side roads leading to resorts. When startled, they rise like a splattering of gold to seek refuge in a nearby tree. Within moments they drop back onto the road to continue feeding.

A few years ago evening grosbeaks were a rarity on the Trail. I first saw them one spring when a handful came to feed on salt that had dripped from my car onto the gravel in the driveway. [1986]

It's time again! Turtles are traveling across the roads to hunt for places to lay their eggs.

81

A few, intent on their mission, have been squashed by speeding cars. One big snapping turtle crawled up beside the blacktop, where it found just the right spot to make a hole and deposit its eggs one by one. After it finished this mission, it covered the hole and paddled down the road.

An interested observer, who had watched the process, picked up the turtle and took it down to the water, where it speedily disappeared.

An indigo bunting sat on a dead birch limb, its solid blue shimmering in the sunlight. The vivid blue shows up so bright against the green background of leaves. Indigo buntings are rarely seen this far north.

SUMMER SOLSTICE SLIPS AWAY. As June slips toward July, I realize the summer solstice has passed.

Each day is getting a few minutes shorter. Our summers are not long and leisurely. Nature has decreed fast growth and fast development.

I have a sudden urge to try to cram into the next couple of months all the fishing, camping and canoeing that I dreamed about during the winter months.

June is gone. Our summer months are so precious. We must savor every moment of July.

JULY

Summer's Sounds

TIME AND AGAIN I HAVE HEARD, "The silence of the forest must not be violated." But can you really imagine a silent forest?

Gone would be the splash of water gurgling along a rocky stream bed or the pounding as it tumbles over a sheer drop to mumble and grind below as it munches on pebbly grain. We would hear no quiet lapping of waves along a lake shore, nor the pulse of water pushed by the wind, reaching ever higher to strike, draw back, lift and strike again.

Silent would be the songbirds who welcome the daylight and put evening to bed. Lost would be the haunting night call of the loon and its soft utterances to its newborn chicks, the sound of ducks gliding to a stop as they splash into the water, the geese gabbling on their migratory flights.

We would be without the whirring of wings as a partridge drums for a mate, the seemingly affectionate murmur that is carried on between the beaver and its babies, and the call and slurp of moose along the water's edge. The music of swamp creatures on a summer night, and woodpeckers tapping on a tree with the breaking dawn would not be heard. The daylong, incessant chatter of squirrels and the song or chiding chirp of chickadees would be muted.

The woods in July are full of high-summer sounds, each telling its own story for those who would listen. Don't violate the silence of the forest? I'd say don't violate the sounds of the forest.

DUCK PORTAGE. Little Rock Falls on the Granite River was known as Escalier (Staircase) at the time of the Voyageurs. The rock portage and rock steps are worn smooth and slightly indented from the tread of many feet over the last hundred years.

The falls descend in three drops, with the final plunge kicking up spume and mist. It is not a high falls, perhaps 20 or 25 feet.

At the top of the falls and to one side is an isolated pool in which a mother mallard and five ducklings splashed and fed on bugs. A dragonfly lit nearby. The mother duck waddled from the pool and scooped it up in a gulp.

The duck continued on across the portage but hesitated at the first rock step. Followed by her brood, she circled back to the top of the falls, where she chose to cross to the opposite shore. As she started across the water, the current became swifter and swifter. The little ones swam mightily until they were literally running across the top of the water. One little fellow was swept over the first drop only to recover, and climb back over a series of rocks to the top.

The mother led her ducklings down a sloping rock into a back eddy pool, shaded by overhanging bushes. The duck and ducklings emerged to slide down a small drop into another pool, where they gathered in a cluster.

The final plunge of water created a misty spume as it tumbled on the rocks below. The mother, followed by her five ducklings, swam out into the mainstream and slid down the last drop with the aplomb of an otter.

Instead of being crashed into broken bodies and scattered feathers, they bobbed up intact, as though emerging from a refreshing shower. [1970]

MAMA MERGANSER. The female merganser sat on the edge of a fallen log that extended into the water. Her rust-colored crest stood upright like a youngster's windblown hair. As we approached she slid into the water and swam back and forth along the shore, occasionally submerging her head and long pointed beak with apparent disinterest in her surroundings.

In time this sleek, colorful hooded merganser again took her post on the sloping log. She checked her surroundings cautiously for a few minutes. Silently and unobtrusively she waddled toward the woods. There she flattened herself on a nest that was surrounded by bits of white down from her body. The incubation period for her eggs is 28 days, and it may be but a short time before she introduces 12 to 14 babies to the water. [1970]

SURVIVAL. In nature there is a continual interplay among the species as they struggle to survive. It carries through in all—animals, birds, and humans.

As Bill Powell of Saganaga Lake was working on a cabin along the lake shore he looked into the water and watched a loon swimming as silently as an alligator, completely submerged except for its eyes.

As Bill watched a baby duck swimming nearby vanished. A short time elapsed and the loon returned to snatch another baby. Bill said he had never before known that a loon was a predator of baby ducks.

Baby loons, which resemble miniature penguins, are excellent swimmers and dive shortly after they take to water. They dive quickly on a signal of alarm, but their endurance while submerged is limited. The gulls have learned the vulnerability of these babies, so they soar across the water and swoop in, first to scatter the family and then to cause a baby loon to dive again and again until it becomes exhausted. With a quick, hard peck, the gulls render the fatal blow. [1971]

RELAY SYSTEM. Messages and pictures these days go miles high to bounce off of Telstar and span the ocean, but NASA, the TV networks and the phone companies don't hold a monopoly on the long-way-around relay systems of this world.

A few days ago a group of girls from Camp Hubert rented four canoes and started a trip on the Granite River. Three canoe loads found the portage around a rapids while the fourth crew missed the portage and found itself in fast water.

As frequently can happen with the inexperienced, the canoeists were lured by a beautiful spume of water that appeared to offer a harmless thrill, but in reality hid a boulder beneath its curl. Down the rapids sailed the whitewater novices and into the crest of the foam with a crunch and sudden stop. The canoe pitched over, dumped the girls and wedged in the rocks. The girls bobbed away from the scene of the crash and arrived at the portage in a manner they had not anticipated.

The three remaining canoes carried the load from there on down the river route to Jock Richardson's on Saganaga Lake. In order to get a message the 10 miles distance as the crow flies to Gunflint Outfitters, Jock had to radio-telephone Port Arthur. People there sent a telegram which traveled via International Falls to Duluth. The telegram message was then telephoned back to the girls' outfitters (the original 10 miles away!) telling the people there of the location of the canoe and the whereabouts of the girls.

Thus the "moccasin telegraph" seems to be replaced by modern communication devices. [1967]

MAROONED. The Gene Malner family of Grand Marais has a cabin on the Canadian side of Saganaga Lake in what is known as Powell's Bay. In the vicinity there is a guardian angel by the name of Irv Benson, who watches over his fold. Before leaving on a trip from the cabin, the Malner contingent usually leaves a note on Irv's door. When Irv comes home, he knows where to hunt for them in case of need. If they return first, they take the note down.

This is a neat arrangement for a prolonged trip, but who doesn't sometimes take a short jaunt without taking proper precautions?

With the men off on a fishing expedition out of Ignace, Ontario, the remaining family members—three women with eight children—were at the cabin by themselves. The kids swam and borrowed oars from the boat to paddle their raft.

That evening, word sifted in that the fishing was good over at the rock pile, which was not far away.

Anglers tossed rods into the boat. One of the responsible girls, Diane, was elected or chose to stay to take care of the little tots, and the three women and older children piled into the boat.

Irene Malner pressed the button on the electric starter and away they went. A few other fishermen were nearby but left shortly after nine. The Malner group stayed on because someone had had a bite. At about ten they decided to go in.

They pulled up the lines and anchor and pressed the starter button. The response was complete silence—not even a grunt. The motor had a hand start, but it took great strength to give the rope the quick snap that would bring the engine to life. Irene's efforts were futile. She wasn't strong enough to give it that quick snap. The oars were still back on the raft where the children had left them. The Malners reanchored and hoped for a rescue.

In the meantime, Diane became worried, left the tiny tots asleep in the cabin and went on a search. She saw a light and encountered some fishermen who advised her to go back home, stay with the children and wait.

In the meantime, the night wore on slowly for the three women with the youngsters, two who were seven and one eleven.

It was Mrs. Robert Stark of Mississippi, and more recently Illinois, who bolstered everyone with her humor. Dawn came, but nary a soul was in sight, so the marooned anglers drifted away from the rock pile and used the anchor as the power for locomotion. By throwing it out and pulling it in—repeating the performance over and over, they made infinitesimal progress.

About eight o'clock, two men in a fishing boat came to their rescue. They hooked on and slowly towed them to Irv Benson's. Irv gave the motor rope a hard flip and it started. Next time the Malners will leave a note. [1972]

ROSES. It's the darnedest thing. Alongside my home are four rose bushes that have been nursed, coddled and covered against cold and snow. They are still struggling just to sprout new leaves, with no buds in sight. Out in the woods, though, the wild roses are already in full bloom. These scent-filled wild bushes thrive.

The Queen Anne's Lace, standing adjacent, is in some instances still encased in two tight leaves that form a cocoon. As the cocoon slowly opens, half of the covering with a curled top knot gives up the green bud clusters reluctantly. When finally released, the clusters soon form a white spreading umbrella. [1969]

HIGH-BUSH CRANBERRY. Along riverbanks the high-bush cranberry (*Ka-wa-we-ag-a-muk* in Chippewa) are in bloom. These bushes have snowy white flowers and small leaves shaped like those of an oak.

Labrador tea can be found in large quantities, a sweep of white extending across the sphagnum moss swamps. This is the time in July when flowers are everywhere—each variety typical to its specific environment. [1968]

TEMPEST AND HER SWALLOWS. In his newsletter, Irv Benson of Saganaga wrote:

We have had a batch of swallows in one of the birdhouses next to the lake. Yesterday, July 11, all of the young ones came out for their first solo flight. Then both young and adults departed about 10 a.m. today. In the afternoon I noticed one remaining swallow poking its head out of the birdhouse. As this had been a common sight for the past week, I thought no more about it. Later in the afternoon Tempest was down by the shore and almost stepped on a young bird that was still in a non-flyable stage. It turned out to be a young swallow. It was simply left behind when it was not as far along in life as the rest of the brood.

Tempest and I hashed over the problem with Mrs. Larkin, a neighbor, and found that the swallow could be fed by poking fried bits of hamburger and mashed egg down its throat with dull tweezers. The bird cooperated by gulping down anything that could be shoved into its mouth. Getting it to open its mouth, though, was somewhat like giving an enema to John Dillinger. We're in hopes that it will survive to the flying stage so it can be sent south when the migration occurs.

It is one of the few Saganaga swallows given a good start in life, courtesy of Matt Johnson's meat and egg department. [1969]

CHICKENS AND DUCKLINGS. At Gunflint Lodge we have a guest from Hungary who at one time had a large farm and raised many chickens. She watched us trying to give some of our adopted baby ducklings to a chicken who had eight chicks of her own.

In Hungary it was customary to feed the mother a little bread soaked in wine (care had to be used not to give too much) and, when the mother was drunk, to slip additional ducklings under her so when she awakened she was not aware she had an enlarged family. It had been our guest's experience that under any other conditions a mother would not take additional babies because otherwise they knew their own young and would reject outsiders. We tried this method, and it worked. [1964]

BOB'S ROBINS. Bob Cushman's road grader was parked and unused, and seemed an ideal place for a robin to establish a nest, lay eggs and hatch its young.

The time came, though, when Bob had to use this equipment.

This also was a time when the young robins had to be fed frequently. I often saw Bob chugging along on his machine with the mother fluttering overhead as the high-riding nest bumped along, securely fastened to the equipment.

I wonder if the chicks ever became seasick, as my kids used to do, riding over the ups and downs of the rocky, gravel-covered roads. [1977]

RALPH AND THE SEVEN LITTLE SQUIRRELS. Ralph Griffis had stored his sleeping bags unrolled. Last week he whipped one off the shelf to roll it up for a canoe trip. Out popped three naked baby squirrels about an inch long. Upon further investigation, he found four more. While he was contemplating their disposal, the mother squirrel arrived with the ferocity of a lion.

She jumped up and down on her hind feet, spit and grabbed the rag with which she was being harassed. She raced up to one baby, took it in her mouth and dashed off. After seven trips she had her family moved to a new unrevealed location, and Ralph was left with a battle-scarred sleeping bag that he said was fit only for his own use. [1969]

GREASY SQUIRREL STUFF. Ellen Zimmerman had a problem. Squirrels persisted in getting to the suet she put out, leaving none of it for the birds she wanted to feed. Ellen watched the squirrels as they climbed the pipe to her feeder with ease. Someone suggested greasing the pipe. Ellen did so. The squirrel climbed and slid. It backed up and took a bigger jump, its feet working frantically. It still did a backslide. It ran up the nearby tree and out on the tip of the branches, but the span to the feeder was too great a leap, so he just sat in the tree and scolded and jawed at anyone who would listen. Now the squirrel has a problem.

MIDSUMMER GETAWAY. From time to time we're fortunate enough to grab a breather in midsummer in the form of a day or an overnight away from home base. So it was that, with Charlotte Merrick as my companion, I went a short way down the Granite River to a midpoint between rapids and falls and set up an overnight camp. The campsite had been left clean—no bottles, no cans, no refuse and a stash of wood nearby.

From a point of land among the thick jack pine came liquid musical sounds that resembled a soft warbling twitter. A number of young swallows were clinging to a perch on a dry stub. The young watched with intense interest as the parent birds circled and swooped, and then the little ones opened their beaks, revealing cavernous yellow openings the parents filled in a flash as they chucked bits of food into the mouths of their young while hovering like hummingbirds. With a flash of blue the parent birds were away again to soar and hunt and glide for another morsel.

The wind rustled the sheltered perch and threw a young one off balance. Instinctively it spread its wings and looked for certain as if it would plop into the water, but just before a calamitous landing, it soared on an updraft and joined the circling adults, suddenly earning its wings and reaching the status of adulthood.

The tree swallow is the only one of this species that sometimes eats seeds and wild berries. All feeding is usually done on the wing, with flying insects forming the bulk of the food. The birds also bathe and drink while on the wing, pausing for an instant to dip to the surface of the water.

Across the inlet from us, in a grassy bay, a doe noiselessly stepped into view. She was a reddish brown, ever on the alert. She ate for a moment, raised her head and looked facing upwind with her long ears pointed forward to catch the slightest sound. She was joined by a spotted fawn who browsed close to her feet and who was affectionately and protectively nudged now and then.

We moved as she turned her head in our direction and she became aware of our presence. It became a contest of who could remain immobile longer. Wariness prevailed. The deer faded into the woods.

Charlotte and I took a quick dip. The surface water was warm, but if we let our feet sink, the water temperature dropped. Drying off on a sunny rock in a protected nook, we watched blue darning needles (dragonflies) zoom from one spot to another. A dragonfly fell to the water and struggled for survival. We reached under it with a long stick; it climbed aboard, slowly dried its wings and flew off for another adventure or to become a meal for the flitting swallows.

A tiny crayfish, as inconspicuous as the submerged brown rock on which it sat, suddenly darted in reverse when a bare foot stepped down in close proximity. I reached down and brought a small snail onto dry rock and watched while it laboriously protruded a portion of its body back toward the water.

Attached to an underwater plant was a tiny red mite. I jiggled the plant and the mite floated away, but I retrieved it in the palm of my hand. When suspended in a single drop of water the mite struggled vainly with its six almost invisible legs. I put it back in the pond where it floated off with the moving water to attach itself to another friendly frond.

A mallard hen with three or four ducklings in tow swam along the shore, under overhanging bushes, as if following channels through a labyrinth of arched bridges. They crossed the sweeping current of a rapids and caught a back eddy in time to ride upstream.

Mergansers sat on an island rock, their reddish-brown crests protruding straight as arrows. A blue heron flapped across the treetops, disappearing to light in a more secluded spot.

With nightfall the fireflies swung their lanterns hither and yon among the trees. A waterfall splashed and dashed its way among the boulders as it had done for eons and may continue to do into eternity.

At midnight the sky became alive with color. The greens, yellows, and reds of the Northern Lights played back and forth, first quick and close, then fading and distant. The sky was studded with the specks of a million stars. The moon sent its beams tiptoeing across the shimmering water. We could only marvel. [1971]

GRIM HARVEST. A small lake once sat like a sparkling jewel, surrounded by a jack pine and spruce forest. It was reached by a woods trail that followed a winding stream dotted by an occasional beaver house and dam. Moose fed on the tubers among the lily pads. All that is changed now.

The forest in this area has been clear-cut. The beaver have been trapped and the dams broken.

Harvesting natural resources is an economic necessity, I am told. The trees, deer, moose, bear, mink, fox, otter, fisher and pine marten must all be harvested. So once were the wolves, caribou, buffalo, eider duck and innumerable other animals and birds.

Nature seldom lends itself to a replanting, for by the time replanting is needed some of the essential ingredients for survival also have been destroyed. When all is harvested, then what? [1973]

CLEAR-CUTTING. I hate clear-cutting. It leaves large areas stripped clean, drastically changes the ecosystem and alters the wildlife habitat. Other types of logging seem to be less drastic.

As I picked raspberries and blueberries along an old logging road my inconsistency struck home. On the one hand, I had difficulty accepting the messiness of a logging operation, even though I was aware that this process let sunlight penetrate to the earth and allow for new growth.

On the other hand, I was perfectly willing to benefit from the side effects of logging. I had been willing to scavenge unused logs or use slabs from a sawmill to supplement my winter wood supply, and I picked berries, which appear primarily after an area has been logged or burned. Who in this country would think of building without using boards?

The area I was in had attracted a number of moose and a few deer. As I had driven along this rocky road with my three-year-old grandson Robert, I had encountered two big bull moose, each with a large spread of antlers still a little fuzzy from the velvet stage. They sauntered down an old brush-covered skid trail.

Robert and I hiked another of those overgrown trails to a blueberry patch that the bears had missed. As we were kneeling on the ground to pick berries, Robert, who had tired of the chore, remarked, "I see something moving—I think it's a moose." I paid no heed for I thought it was no doubt his imagination's carryover from the moose we had previously seen.

There was a moment of silence and then an awed voice, "Gran, I'm scared." I looked up, and there, about 60 feet from us, stood a large cow moose who was watching us with interest.

The moment led me to realize that it was there because it was a new-growth area. The new aspen, interspersed with some pine, was only about shoulder high. In the past, this country had thick stands of mature jack pine mixed with tall aspen. Somehow I had failed to let that picture vanish so I could focus on a stand of new timber in the making.

Another time I had walked through a forest—or, to be more literal, I had climbed over fallen and dead timber that had passed its prime—and in this jumble was a minimum of new growth. It was a veritable tinderbox.

I came to the conclusion that saving the wilderness for future generations, as some have proposed, is like saving old, ailing, diseased and tired people for the younger generation to behold.

More realistically, perhaps we should allow small chunks of timber to be harvested, apart from recreational areas, to create a mix of the young with the old so that game can seek protection among the older trees and at the same time derive nourishment from the new growth. Only the exceptions, say where certain trees live to be 300, 500 and 1,500 to 2,000 years old, should be retained as a special heritage.

Is it the 50-year growing period we cannot face—a time of trees to no trees, to young trees, to mature trees again? Or should the trees be consumed by fire and not harvested, with their ashes serving as a nutrient for new growth?

Through the eons there has been a slow but constant change—of people, animals, fish, trees, flowers, mountains. There is a wearing away and dying and changing of habitat. Without renewal by replanting, or the slower natural process of the forest, there would be no wilderness.

The moose slowly walked by us and disappeared among the trees. [1977]

LOSSES OF PETRA AND CHARLIE BOOSTROM. When Petra Boostrom left us, we lost one of our most distinguished pioneers. Way back when we had a single-grounded circuit telephone line hung precariously on trees as our only talking link to town, it was Petra we turned to. It took two or three parties cranking at the same time on our magneto-powered phones to get an impulse over the long line from Gunflint to Grand Marais. With Clearwater being at the halfway point invariably Petra was called upon.

There was always a cheery response: "Wait a minute until I tie a baby in the chair, shove the food back on the stove (it was heated with wood) and then I'll help."

Petra raised a large family and cooked for resort guests. When the Depression hit and we were all mighty hard-pressed there was always room at her table for an extra person or two, some of whom stayed on and on.

During the fires of 1936, when Charlie was on the fire line for over a solid month, Petra ran the resort single-handedly.

She was always there with sage advice, too. There was the time I went through the ice on Daniels Lake with the dog team and barely got out. As I drove the remaining team into Clearwater in a pair of pajamas and was somewhat shook, Petra greeted me with, "Well now, that was a bit close, but come in and warm up and have a cup of coffee and a slice of fresh bread."

The eulogy could go on and on from a thousand people. [1976]

Charlie Boostrom, at 91, a true Gunflint Trail pioneer, has died.

He originally homesteaded on Moon Lake and at one time had an extensive trapline. With an ax and a knife he could create many things. He built log cabins as well as the present Clearwater log lodge, furniture, docks and canoe paddles. He could split rocks with the swing of a heavy rock hammer and a scarcely audible grunt. He could create from a pile of rocks a fireplace or a rock home.

When the railroad was being built from Cascade to Rose Lake he ran a construction camp. He drove dogs, hauling supplies for survey crews in the winter. When the roads were plugged with snow, as they frequently were in those days, Charlie drove his dog team to town for supplies.

He fought forest fires for a solid month in 1936, the last year of our bad fires. To him I am forever grateful, for when Gunflint Lodge burned at the end of June in 1953, it was to Charlie I turned.

I suppose he might have been considered a competitor, for he and Petra operated Clearwater Lodge. When I asked for his help in getting a new foundation started for another lodge building he looked down at me with his sharp but kindly blue eyes, shifted his tobacco from one cheek to the other, let go with a spat and said, "What are we waiting for? We'll start tomorrow."

With pride of workmanship and accomplishment, and without coffee breaks, toilet breaks, smoke breaks, clock watching or the eight-hour day, he led his crew (Chris Broton and Frank Horak, who had lost an arm in a sawing accident). With plans sketched on a piece of wrapping paper he built our new lodge. Charlie returned the following year and built the two fireplaces.

He was a man of compassion and no nonsense. They don't make them like that anymore. [1979]

BEAR TALES. At East Bearskin the Cavanaughs have a pet bear that comes to their doorstep each day. There have been a couple of other rambunctious bears around who have damaged campers' equipment. The question centered on how to remove the bears that were causing trouble without harming the pet.

The pet bear's name is Junior, and the problem has been solved. Recently while Junior had his head deep in a garbage can, one of the gals from Bearskin Lodge swatted him on the rump with a brush of yellow paint. Now we'll know Junior when we see him. [1968]

Someone suggested that if mothballs were scattered across a bear path, the bears would dislike the odor and turn back. Meticulously mothballs were strung across the face of a dump site where over-eager bears refused to wait for the cans to be pulled from the trucks and dumped. The mothballs glistened white like a string of well-placed pearls.

Almost immediately twin bear cubs appeared to investigate the mothballs and gobble them up. If anyone else encounters a young bear with a mothball-smelling burp, you can be assured he came from the Gunflint dump. [1970]

Other animals besides just birds and squirrels like the seeds that many of us set out.

At one of the resorts, a full sack of sunflower seeds was sitting on the back porch—that is until it was discovered by a yearling bear. This frequent visitor arrived one evening, plucked all of the hanging suet put out for the birds and then picked up the sack of seeds in its front arms and, standing upright, waddled down the path.

SUMMER SLIPS AWAY. Summer is slipping by. Baby loons are no longer riding on their mother's back but have acquired a teen-age look. Young birds have left their nests. Raspberry season has ended. The beavers have started to drag in their winter food supply. Gee whiz! Where are my dreamed-up summer canoe trips?

AUGUST

Forest Abundance

IT'S ALL OUT THERE. All you have to do is make the harvest, like the other creatures of the forest.

The blueberries are abundant this year if you can get there ahead of other two- and four-legged creatures. This is one of those rare summers with no tent catepillars and just enough warmth and moisture to develop large, lush berries. But the bears love them at least as much as we do.

Flowers have burst into color. There is the purple of the aster, white Queen Anne's lace, coral butter and eggs, and bunchberry.

The forest floor is carpeted with an assortment of mushrooms. Their lids may be buff or pink, yellow or white. On the underside of the mushroom umbrella, thin, ribbon-like gills are spaced precisely.

What appear at first glance to be white flecks of birch bark, on closer examination are clumps of Indian pipes with nodding flowers. These waxy, fragile saprophytic plants have appeared beside the stiff brown seed pods from another year.

Have you really looked?

This is August. There is so much to see.

THANK HEAVENS. There are times when a resorter likes to sneak off for a day and, if particularly lucky, camp overnight. So it happened.

We went to a lake that was off the beaten path and quite isolated—and chock-full of northerns. A pair of bald eagles circled and landed on the topmost branch of a tree. Their white heads and tails stood out in stark contrast to their dark wings and bodies.

We paddled toward a beaver house and cast among the brush. A northern rose to the bait, jumped to shake itself loose and made a long run. A successful retrieve brought us our dinner. To take a fish for food just a short time before it graces the frying pan is the ultimate outdoors experience.

A Finn Heddon spinner bait proved the most enticing. We caught and released one fish after another.

White lilies rode gracefully on the ripples made by our canoe. As the flowers bobbed back and forth they brushed a fallen log. A loon suddenly called frantically and went through a series of swooping gyrations—first almost erect out of water, then skidding along its breast and then rising again. I wondered if a northern hadn't just snatched the

loon's young, for I have seen these tactics when the loons were trying to draw the attention of predators away from their babies.

We found a delightful small island for our tent, and a kind breeze wafted the mosquitoes away. A full moon gradually poked its way over the treetops and then seemed to rise hurriedly in the sky.

As we lay on the rocks which were still warm from the day's sun, we watched a satellite cross the sky. It scurried rapidly, at times obscured by some high misty clouds, to reappear farther on and shortly vanish.

The next morning we decided to follow a trapper's trail that meandered from one beaver pond to another.

The trail through the wooded area was accented by moose and deer tracks, and occasionally bear spoor. Alongside one grassy waterway a deer as brown as a dead cedar stood and watched us with interest and, after drinking leisurely, turned and vanished.

At an opening where the water bubbled over some rocks we too leaned down for a drink. Just a few feet away—unseen by us—a beaver slipped into the water and then announced our presence with such a resounding slap of its tail that it sprinkled our heads with water.

We crossed a long grassy meadow that had once been a beaver pond. Now it was a friendly meeting place for moose, for along the way we counted 10 moose beds. One group of animals had been a family of four, but the rest were all singletons.

Farther along the area became a little more marshy. Here were literally acres of purple wild iris. The blossoms were slightly past prime, but the field was startling in its beauty. Innumerable drops of gold were in the grass, perhaps it was field cinquefoil.

Overhead a turkey vulture soared and rode the air currents.

A tamarack swamp revealed purple vetch—pitcher plants with their round, green faces turned toward the sun. The leaves surrounding their faces made them look like jesters.

There were so many things to see along this trail as it wound through the woods and along and across creeks. There were blueberries (small for lack of rain); raspberries, plentiful and delicious; thimbleberries and high-bush cranberries. We encountered wild currants and dogberries that were just acquiring a tinge of blue. Indian pipe, white and ghostly, stood among red amanita mushrooms and green horsetails.

We came upon a stand of towering white ash that appeared to be about eighty feet high, and a cedar with a girth of five or six feet. These were reminders of the trees that were plentiful in these parts before they were logged or scoured by fire.

We shuffled through a carpet of mint that sent a pleasant aroma through the air. We went through a stand of diamond willow. At one time this wood was used locally to make handcrafted furniture but now it is found in only a few places in the woods.

In one stretch on our trek all the birch and pine trees we saw had burls. With painstaking hand work, burls from the birch can be made into bowls and cups and saucers. When the burls are sanded and polished, their colors and swirls are exotic.

There are those who look and enjoy all these intricacies of nature, and then there are those, like a lady who swooped into our lodge recently, who remarked, "My—I was here 25 years ago, and it is still the same God-forsaken place it was then."

I remarked, "Thank heavens."

She stalked out. [1966]

NORTHERN LIGHTS. Starting from a cone overhead, rays of light extended in all directions. In the north slowly waving curtains of light changed shape constantly. The full moon was tinted on the lower edge with pale pinks and greens. As the display reached its peak it suddenly vanished, leaving in its wake a clear starlit sky, a brilliant moonbeam on the water and the solitary call of a loon. [1959]

The Northern Lights have started their fall displays. On Monday night these lights wavered softly across the horizon, extending their stage from the hills to the Big Dipper and accentuated by a series of beamed footlights. The heavens were studded with twinkling stars—the audience in this open-air amphitheater, spectators who perched, watchful and appreciative. [1961]

A CANOE TRIP TO THE QUETICO. Four gray-haired (salt and pepper is a nicer term) women decided on a canoe trip.

Charlotte Merrick, Doris Krebsbach, Eleanor "Mat" Matsis and I were the principals involved. The starting point was a fly-in to Powell Lake, at the northeastern edge of the Quetico.

We paddled down the serpentine Greenwood River to the Ka-wa-we-aga-muck and stopped for a couple of days at Mack Lake. (The Indian name for the river means high-bush cranberry. I suspect that was too much for the printers, so it had been shortened on maps to Wa-wi-ag.)

It is my contention that fish should be caught to eat and beyond that point are best served by leaving them swimming in the lake. A few hours of fishing in Mack Lake and we had walleyes for lunch, supper and breakfast.

As we paddled on down the Wa-wi-ag, we met a group of teen-agers with older leaders riding amidship. They were from Sommers Canoe Base. In a puzzled sort of way they asked what group we were with. We answered that we were a sewing circle of the Geriatric Society making an exploratory trip for those who might follow. We could recommend it as an excellent cure for arthritis, bursitis, backaches, sciatic nerve pinches and stiff joints. [1973]

Why is it that every lake that you come to entices you to stay on and explore bays and marshes for moose or beaver?

We took the route of the six falls. As a result of the bountiful rains, there was a heap of water pouring, tumbling and jostling down precipitous drops. Mat looked at one swift slick that ended in a dancing froth and remarked, "That would be a No. 10 Rapids (toughest on a scale of 10) in the Grand Canyon."

En route we had stopped at Wet Lake for a couple of nights and caught an abundance of bass. They always rise and jump free of the water when hooked and then often break loose.

It was here we met a couple from Kentucky who make a canoe trip to the Quetico every summer. They were accompanied by a white poodle. In a pronounced Southern drawl the woman slowly remarked, "Y'all look at my dawg. He's a registered purebred and he jest flopped in the mud to cool. Y'all without a man? You're brave."

After 85 miles and 15 portages it was a seasoned crew who camped on Saganagons before taking the beaver pond route to Saganaga.

PORTAGES GO TO POT. Paddling down a narrow, weedy lake recently we came across a large bed of water lilies whose outermost petals were a deep pink. A sweet fragrance filled the air.

Once we could reach these places over good portages with trails and docks built and maintained by the state government. Maps were not as accurate as they are now, but names of the lakes and the portage distances were on signs at the

beginning of each trail. Hewn logs, replaced when needed, covered marshy areas.

But then various public-property landholdings were con- solidated. In many places state lands were swapped for federal lands and vice versa. In our area the swap resulted in a concentration of federal property.

As the federal bureaucracy took over, trail and dock main- tenance ceased, and directional signs were forgotten. This group of government employees didn't have any use for the logs at hand, either. It was their contention that trails should be allowed to revert to the natural state.

Logs that once served as pathways through marshy areas now lie half rotted. The footing is precarious. Docks installed years ago now offer exposed spikes and collapsed planks in mute evidence of their neglect. [1963]

BEAR TALES. Several guests from Gunflint Lodge drove to the Hungry Jack open dump in hopes of seeing bears. Their wishes were granted as a couple of large bears ambled across the road and worked over the available tidbits. The guests fumbled for their cameras and eased the car back a little and then forward to get a better view.

On a nearby hill a bear sat watching them with interest. As the gals made the final move to get a perfect picture, they heard an ominous hissing sound as one rear tire slowly deflated. The bear on the hill, 25 or 30 feet away, stretched out to enjoy the spectacle.

Darkness descended. No flashlight! One of the women shakily eased out of the car with a wavering cigarette lighter to check the tire. Still flat. While the bear watchers worried how long they would sit before someone from Gunflint came searching for them, the crew from Gateway Lodge happened along. They changed the tire in a jiffy.

Neatly embedded in the wall of the tire was the sharp bone of a T-bone steak. The crew from Gateway claimed it was from one of their delicious steaks. The gals from Gunflint observed that the Gateway guests must have nibbled the bones mighty close, even working the ends to a point. [1958]

Nat Rusk of Seagull Lake had finished baking a blueberry pie and had stepped outside to pick a bouquet of flowers for the table. As she returned and entered the kitchen she was confronted with a two-and-a-half or three-year old bear—literally face to face.

Nat let out a scream for her husband, Ken, that should have lifted the roof and rolled the bear back on its haunches, but didn't. Nat made a fast retreat to the shop where Ken was working with ear protectors on and had a machine buzzing. He had heard nothing.

Together they returned to the house to find the bear. It had torn off the patio screendoor and was standing and poking around, wondering what all the excitement was about. The bear had not consumed the pie. [1984]

Margaret Nolan of Sunset Lodge on Hungry Jack made a short sortie to the "chick sales" behind their cabin. Upon emerging from the two-holer Margaret was confronted by a large bear who calmly stretched across the path in a reclining position. Margaret was trapped and retreated to her shelter. The bear watched with interest every move she made.

Hours later Harry came home for his supper. After many shouts for his wife, he heard a desperate call: "Out back!"

He ran for his gun and scared off the bear. They wondered if the bear had been waiting his turn to use the biffy. Margaret was relieved to be freed from her confining quarters. [1959]

COMPASSION. We hear so much of worldwide meanness that it is refreshing to hear about kindnesses that are so often extended and so seldom recognized. Mr. Ryan, his wife and four children, after outfitting at the Gunflint Northwoods

Outfitters, were on Rose Lake on their canoe trip. Mr. Ryan chopped his hand severely. A group from the Menogyn YMCA camp came by and helped the parents and two smallest children over portages and back to the road. The 10- and 12-year-old Ryans were left at the campsite with all of the gear and one canoe.

By chance the Larsons of Windigo Lodge, out for an afternoon drive, stopped at the landing as the Ryans came in. They loaded the family in their car and took them to Gunflint. Guides were dispatched to go after the youngsters and their gear, while the Larsons took the Ryans to the hospital in Grand Marais.

In the meantime the two youngsters dismantled the camp, packed up all the gear, loaded it in the remaining canoe, paddled to the Rose Lake portage and had everything toted to the top of Stairway Portage, except the canoe, when the Gunflint guides appeared.

The concern and thoughtfulness extended by the group from Menogyn, by the Larsons of Windigo and by their outfitters overwhelmed the Ryans. They said that had they been in trouble back home in Chicago, people would have bypassed them and gone merrily on their way.

Because giving a helping hand is not the exception in these parts, what particularly impressed us was the resourcefulness of these two city youngsters. I have no doubt that given enough time they would have moved the canoe up the rise, step by step. Their effort was outstanding, because we often hear stalwart young men remark about the toughness of this particular portage. [1968]

GRANITE RIVER ARTIFACTS. Last week a couple of divers with the Minnesota Historical Society did some additional exploring in the Granite River. This trip proved to be as productive as others have been. Among their finds was a clay pipe complete with stem, the first unbroken pipe recovered;

a dagger, the type worn on a belt; a shoe buckle; trade beads; an instrument used to strike flint to start a fire; the seal used on bundles of trade goods (complete with decipherable numbers and insignia); a bundle of spears; a chunk of orange ocher (from France) used in paintings; and a number of small, unidentified articles. Many of the artifacts will eventually be placed in the museum at Grand Portage. [1964]

TRAPPED. Charlie Ott was once a game warden and is now semi-retired. We call him Trapper Ott these days. He has had a difficult time trying to catch a couple of chipmunks that persist in peeking from around corners at the Grand Marais Outfitters, where he works.

First Charlie tried a couple of live traps baited with peanut butter and jelly tidbits. The chippies peeked from the corners, walked around and over the traps and went their merry, scurrying way. In frustration Charlie set a trap outside the door, which seemed to be on the chipmunk path.

In the morning Trapper Ott was notified that a good trapper should check his traps early.

Charlie queried with apprehension, "A skunk?"

The answer was, "No, just a fur piece for your wife."

As Charlie approached the live trap, he heard a "meow" and faced a little brown kitten. [1968]

Harry Nolan had a mink trap set under a boat at Poplar Lake. Floyd Soderberg, in his meanderings around the place, discovered animal tracks that he analyzed as those belonging to a bobcat or lynx. The tracks led in the trap's direction.

Following the tracks, Floyd discovered they led under the boat. Upon hearing the rattling of the trap, he became excited over the catch he was about to make.

He hurried back to the cabin and called the Nolans. Harry wasn't home. He called his neighbors, the Millers, for advice, but they weren't home, either, so he called the Nolans again.

This time Mrs. Nolan answered and advised that he pull the trap out carefully and hit the animal over the head. A gun was inappropriate unless it was deemed advisable to shoot a hole in the boat.

Floyd got a long pipe, went back to the hidden trap, pulled the chain gingerly and, as the head started to protrude, he socked it with the pipe. Great was his chagrin when he discovered that the lynx he had just killed was none other than Sammy. Sammy was a Siamese cat, a lady of 4 years who was kind to children and never scratched. Sammy's home was at Balsam Grove Resort.

STEALING. About 10 days ago a group camped at American Point on Saganaga Lake. Their six tents were placed within a small area. During their stay they took a day to explore and fish. Upon their return they found all of their tents had been stolen. Their food, packs, sleeping bags and cooking utensils were left intact.

I have heard it said that the people who once occupied these lands were uneducated and primitive. They maintained a social code, however, that ensured that trapping shacks throughout the entire forest were left unlocked and would remain undisturbed. The cabins often contained a gun, snowshoes, food staples, sleeping bags, traps and a toboggan or two.

As the present civilization, with a different set of values, encroaches, the old way of life is no longer possible. A trapping shack would be stripped of its contents in a couple of weeks. [1974]

FIRES! It all started midway between Red Rock Bay, which extends south from Saganaga Lake, and Alpine Lake, about a half mile inland from the canoe route. It appeared to be a result of a lightning strike. With the lack of rain the woods were vulnerable, and a stubborn fire followed.

As the fire traveled toward Gunflint Lake all available firefighters were called in. A west wind persisted, and the lines had to drop back. Water-bombing planes carried on continuous missions, while small observation planes circled and spotted new danger points.

At Grandad Lake four local fellows on one of the first crews had to take to the water. They clung to a log as the fire jumped the lake as if it wasn't even there.

The fire moved toward Gull Lake and the river, where a new line was established. Local crews were relieved by bus loads of firefighters recruited by the government. A kitchen unit was established at the Sea Guard Station. The resorts contributed with boats, motors and food for the firefighting crews.

The fire also jumped Sea Gull River at the rapids and started fires in the campsite area. The resorts, outfitters and the Plymouth Youth Camp were all in vulnerable locations.

The following morning the wind switched to the northeast, which caused the fire to burn back on itself and become less dangerous to the threatened homes and business establishments. The north bay of Sea Gull, immediately to the west of the river, became a desolate burned-out stretch, along with the nearby islands.

One man, in utter frustration, tried to put out a fire at a beautiful green point by pouring buckets of water on it. It was hopeless. Later I saw him pouring water on his shoes, for he had found the ground hotter than he had expected.

As it became evident that the campground would have to be evacuated, one man sitting in his lawn chair before his tent refused to move. He appeared to be enjoying the spectacle of watching the forest burn. The foresters moved him.

The final exodus of campers and residents from that area made the narrow Gunflint Trail, for a short time, look like the freeway in the Twin Cities—outbound on a Friday night.

At the end of the week the wind ripped out of the west and

whipped the lakes a frothy white. The wind made it impossible for planes to drop water-bombs. Had this wind developed at the height of the fire, nothing could have held it back. It was purely a gift from the spirits that people didn't lose their homes and businesses.

Still, that vast area of 2,000 acres was largely burned out, although as you drive up the Trail you don't see any evidence of the fire. It is only on certain portions of the shore along Sea Gull Lake and Red Rock Bay that the fire damage is evident, and even there, many green pockets are left.

The inner portion of the circle, however, burned hard and clean. It was the efforts of a crew from Wilderness Canoe Base that saved the palisades on Sea Gull Lake. [1976]

A WHITE SIGHT. Russell Blankenburg was gazing at what he thought was an albino blue heron. He hurried to the cabin to tell Eve, who thought he was kidding. (Incidentally, Russell has a quick walk that belies his 85 years). "If you don't believe me, just go look. It's by your garden," he said.

Eve eased over that way, and there stood a white egret, complete with orange bill and black legs, wading at the water's edge. Russell wasn't far off, for the egrets were once also known as great white herons. When their plumage was popular for hat decorations, they were almost exterminated.

A guest from Gunflint Lodge watched the same white bird fly east down the lake. Egrets are rare in these parts. [1980]

THE CASE OF THE WAYWARD COMPASS. Elizabeth, one of the naturalists on the Gunflint Lodge staff, took a day's trip on a portion of the Granite River. On one of the portages she lost her compass.

A few days later Eve Blankenburg and I went that route to pick blueberries. We set a couple of filled buckets off at the lower end of the same portage while we negotiated the rapids in the canoe. Although the rapids were of no real consequence, there is always the remote chance of a slip that could cause a loss.

When I walked back to retrieve the berry pails I noticed a pair of jeans partially covered with mud from the flowage. Upon closer inspection they appeared to be almost new. Eve squeezed them out, and we plopped them in our canoe.

Back at the Lodge, I flopped the jeans over a line and promptly forgot about them.

A day or so later I glanced at Elizabeth and said, "I found a pair of jeans in the water and the waist looks about your size. Maybe you could use them." She tried them on and found they fit her perfectly. As she jammed her hand in the pocket she encountered something hard. It was her compass, with her identification mark on it. As she pulled it out, the pocket lining turned inside out and revealed the name "Bob" printed on the inside pocket.

It all falls into place. Elizabeth lost her compass. Bob, whoever he was, found it. Bob lost his pants, and I found them. Elizabeth tried on the pants and found her compass. One of those weird round robins. [1980]

RESCUES. On Gunflint Lake four fellows from St. Paul had been fishing in Magnetic Bay with their catamaran canoes and motor. They came through the narrows, headed across the lake and encountered a gusty blow. They started to ship water but kept plowing into the waves, gradually losing their steerage.

Gene and Jane Gasper, Gunflint summer-home owners, along with two other guests, had left their home to go down the lake with their sizable boat and 25-horse motor. From afar they noticed the predicament. The canoes were swamped, and four panic-stricken men were in the water. Two of the men couldn't swim, and, among them, they had one life jacket.

Gene motored his boat up to the canoes and hauled aboard

three of the men—making seven in the Gasper boat—and retrieved most of the equipment, except for a camera and one fishing pole.

A fisherman chanced by and picked up the fourth man. The Gaspers tied onto the swamped canoes and, in the face of more squalls, towed the outfit to the dock at Gunflint Lodge.

No one from Gunflint or Borderland Lodge had seen the accident that had taken place or they, too, would have helped in the rescue.

Most canoeists do not have the wisdom of the Indians, who paddled close to shore, where their odds for safety were the greatest and where they would see the most animal and bird activity. [1980]

TORNADO. We have known winds to come through and take a swath of trees, knocking them down as if they were jackstraws, but a tornado that spirals down and concentrates on a pinpoint is a rarity here.

It was one of those warm, lazy days that makes you want to go for a swim and cool off. About supper time Pat and Frank Shunn took a leisurely swim and then ambled back to their cabin, which is built on a promontory overlooking Saganaga Bay.

As they sauntered up the steps to the cabin they noticed that ominous silence that sometimes precedes a weather change. In this silence the birds are still and the squirrels and chipmunks stop chattering. You get an eerie sensation. Perhaps it is from such feelings that superstitions are born.

As Frank walked across the living room an unexpected wind sprang up. A clap of thunder shook the house, followed by another. In the stunning noise and gales Frank and Pat felt as if they were standing on a track with a bullet train headed straight for them. The house shuddered and wrenched. The window over the kitchen sink shattered, and flying glass shot across the room. The wall containing the sinks and cupboards moved in about four inches, severing all of the water and drain lines.

Outside, white pines two and a half feet in diameter and 80 feet tall—grand trees that had stood for 250 to 300 years—were uprooted and knocked prone.

In the house's electric service panel, fortunately, the circuit breakers had functioned, so the risk of a fire was lessened, but lights and all electrical appliances were rendered dark and still.

As the attack waned Pat stepped to the door to survey the damage. The steps were gone. The boardwalk, the ramp and several gas tanks had been slammed against the roots of a tremendous upturned pine that had stood beside the house.

Pat and Frank went out the front door onto a porch from which they could crawl to a rock ledge and over the fallen pine to see if their truck was intact. It wasn't. A huge tree had fallen across the top, squashing the cab. Nearby other huge pines had been uprooted. In the midst of this mess, on top of a rounded rock, sat the snowmobile, untouched.

The tornado, as it formed and spiraled down, was seen by Bob Lewis, who was watching the spectacle from his house. He had planned to leave that day for a flight to Alaska but had been advised to stay put, as there was weather brewing. He had his plane buoyed off the shore when the storm hit. He watched the boathouse shake and tremble and 35 trees come crashing down. The wind didn't hit his plane, but tore by a few feet away. He watched the plane rock quietly, like a canoe riding a backwater below a turbulent rapids.

The storm was all over within minutes and, after a short squall, the sun reappeared, and the squirrels and chipmunks came out, demanding food. [1983]

POISON IVY CURE. An acquaintance sent me a sample of the plant used by Indians in Wisconsin as a cure for poison ivy.

In my attempt to identify the plant I got bogged down in technical terms, so I buzzed down the road to Ken and Molly Hoffman for help. I quote their answer:

"The plant in question is called sweetfern (*Comptonia peregrina*). It is not a fern, but a deciduous shrub. It grows to a height of five feet under ideal conditions and produces nut-like fruits. Traditionally it has been used to make tea (as far back as the American Revolution). The plant prefers dry soils and old fields where it often grows in masses. It is found from Manitoba to Nova Scotia and south to Virginia and Illinois."

According to the Indians, sweetfern should be gathered in August, boiled in water and strained. The liquid is put in jars, where it will keep unrefrigerated until it is opened. Then it must be refrigerated. I am told that when the liquid is applied to a poison ivy infection it stops the itching and spreading and dries up the infection. [1983]

CHIEF SEATTLE. Chief Seattle of the Nez Perce Tribe from the state of Washington sent the following letter to President Franklin Pierce in 1855. It is worth quoting for it fits the feeling of many people who live on the Trail, year-round or part-time:

The great chief in Washington sent word that he wishes to buy our land. How can you buy or sell the warmth of the land? Every part of the earth is sacred to my people. Every shiny pine needle, every shady shore, every mist in the dark woods, every clearing and humming insect is holy in the memory of my people.

We know that the white man does not understand our ways. One portion of the land is the same to him as the next for he is a stranger who comes in the night and takes from the land whatever he needs. The earth is not his brother but his enemy, and when he has conquered it, he moves on. He leaves his father's grave, and his children's birthright is forgotten.

There is no quiet place in the white man's cities. No place to hear the leaves of spring or the rustle of insect wings.

But perhaps, because I am savage and do not understand, the clatter only seems to insult the ears.

And what is there to life if a man cannot hear the lovely cry of the whippoorwill or the argument of the frog around the pool at night?

The whites, too, shall pass, perhaps sooner than other tribes. Continue to contaminate your own bed and you will one night suffocate in your own waste.

When the buffalo are all slaughtered, the wild horses are tamed, the secret corners of the forest heavy with the scent of many men and the view of the ripe hills blotted by talking wires—where is the thicket? Gone.

Where is the eagle? Gone.

And what will it be to say goodbye to the swift and the hunt? It will be the end of living and the beginning of survival.

AUTUMN SIGNS.   A summer-home owner stopped in at Trail Center and complained that there were no birds this year.

At Trail Center alone they have had eight families nesting close to the buildings and water's edge. There were flickers, robins, waxwings, chipping sparrows, kingbirds, myrtle warblers, sapsuckers and blackbirds all busily feeding their young. The swallows, white-throated sparrows, Canadian jays and a family of hummingbirds have been nesting and raising their families.

Now, though, indications of the beginning of fall have appeared. Wave upon wave of warblers—black and white,

myrtles and some that looked like Tennessee warblers—
passed through. They signaled the beginning of a migratory
movement. One minute they were everywhere, and a few
minutes later they had vanished. [1982]

A snowy owl came swooping in from the north. The traffic
controller gave the wrong signal, and the owl smacked into
the chimney at the Wickes' house on Gunflint Lake. When
the Wickses heard the crash, they thought a tree limb had hit
the roof, and they went out to see what had happened. They
discovered the owl.

It was sitting on the ground, stunned, disoriented and
dizzy. This was one time when an owl posed quietly to have
its picture taken from every angle. After about 15 minutes of
being admired this northern owl tired of all the mug shots,
hopped up on a limb and gracefully lifted away to meld into
the forest. [1986]

This time of year a little fire in the fireplace wards off a
chill. Sometimes the smoke will surprise you by curling
everywhere in the house but up the chimney. Recently when
such an event occurred it was discovered that a chimney
swift had glued its nest against the inner wall of the stack.
With a little prying the nest came tumbling down into the
hearth intact.

Close examination revealed a work of art, or more aptly a
lesson in adaptation. The crescent shaped nest was built of
short sturdy twigs fastened together with a shiny glutinous
material that held the parts firmly. The three or four eggs that
were to be deposited in this confined space must have been
tiny.

On a recent drive down the Gunflint Trail at the break of
dawn the morning mist wafted across the road. The veil-like
shroud covered the lakes that I passed. Here and there a

breeze brushed aside the blanket of fog to reveal a tall pine anchored to a rocky point.

As I made my way down the Trail the sun grew higher and hotter. The mist thinned and vanished in the new light, revealing the clear lakes and their tree-lined shores in quiet beauty.

This cool morning softness was signaling those who were alert to prepare for the next change of seasons.

SEPTEMBER

Autumn's Carpet

THE COLORING OF AUTUMN starts now. Ferns turn a soft buff. Bushes and brush along the road assume various shades of yellow.

Aspen and birch trees are freckled with green and yellow leaves, and the occasional moose maple bush or maple tree stands out in a flash of red. Mountain ash are loaded with fresh berries—a feast for fall and winter birds.

A weaver is creating a colorful carpet for the forest floor with an intricate pattern of gold and red intermingled among deep greens, pastel browns and purples. With a light tug the gentle wind scatters the colors. Each new layer of leaves gently descends to take its place among the thick padding of mosses and berries.

Fall brings on a restlessness in us all. We recognize this feeling in other creatures with our sighting of a moose in search of a mate or a shorebird on its southward flight.

This yearly cycle reminds me of the span of life. The leaves emerge in the spring, fresh, dancing and trembling with eagerness, and then gradually mature and become more robust. They bend and swing with the forces of summer. In the fall they reach the zenith of their careers and begin reflecting the mellowness and colorful contribution of their lifetimes. And then gradually they go, their generation to be replaced by those that follow.

LYNX FORCE. Canadian lynx have moved into the area with force. Since April first of this year game wardens have paid more than a hundred bounties on lynx. Forty-two have been caught by Pete Peterson. In all the years that Art Johnson has been game warden he cannot remember such an influx of these animals. This may be one reason why there are fewer partridge this year compared to previous years.

A flock of ducks on Pike Lake had a close encounter. At Rudy Backlund's place a group of people were feeding these ducks, as they had been all summer, when a lynx pounced into their midst and grabbed a duck. In its hurry to make its escape the lynx dropped the duck, which flew off unhurt.

As the crowd was recovering from this surprise attack the lynx was back for another try, but this time the spectators were more composed, and the animal was shot.

These animals have moved in to feed on squirrels, rabbits, partridge and other small animals. They appear to ingest them whole and then regurgitate the undigestible parts. I have been told they feed on lemmings, too. It may have been a shortage of that food supply that drove them down to our area. [1963]

MUSHROOMING. The woods are bursting with mushrooms of all sizes and varieties. Where two days ago there appeared to be only the decayed humus of the pine needles and logs, the slumbering earth has sprung to life with little umbrellas of white, red, yellow and buff.

Some mushrooms look like flower petals flecked with brown. Whole patches of yellow fluted shoots appear. Possibly they are spores of some kind of other mushrooms still undeveloped. Along the top of a rotting log a mass of edible puffballs stands erect. [1959]

HONKERS. Several flocks of geese have started their southward flights. The wavering V formations, sometimes high and sometimes low at daybreak or in the late afternoon, are accompanied by the unforgettable sound of the honkers as they carry on their incessant chatter.

For we who are earthbound the movement of the geese arouses a dormant instinct, dating back eons. We want to rise and sail away to other lands; to cross mountains and valleys and lakes; to gaze down on neatly checkered farms, small towns and the cities that flow in all directions; to be free of wars and race riots, bickering and strife.

As the spirit soars with that yen to go reality keeps us rooted to earth. [1967]

REPORTS FROM THE BWCA. Canoeists have probed every crevice and stream of the Boundary Waters Canoe Area. Conversations that we have overheard reveal their stories, their opinions, the adjustments that have been suddenly thrust upon them.

One woman, who was visiting from a city with heavy traffic, found the deep silence of the woods at night almost unbearable. But then, who of us having suddenly moved from the silence of the woods to the noise of a metropolitan sports show and the stuffiness of a big-city hotel room hasn't found this a difficult adjustment, too?

Another canoeist was not happy until her husband built a wooden bough shelf for their camp so all items could be arranged in an orderly manner.

There was a man who swam in a quiet bay and was joined by a mink and an otter. There were those who hurried through the country to tell of the number of portages they covered and the lakes they paddled across. There were also those who took a more leisurely pace and encountered a family of otters who challenged the paddlers over territorial rights.

Canoeists have reacted to the new regulations of "no bottles and no cans in the Boundary Waters Canoe Area" with their overwhelming approval and almost universal cooperation.

Most of the canoe outfitters had been advocating and using dehydrated foods, instead of canned foods, for several years. It was not because the outfitters were emerging as environmentalists, but because they were always seeking ways to lighten the loads and keep campsites cleaner for their customers. [1971]

PEGGY'S FRIENDS. As the dawn infringed upon the darkness of a moonless night Goldfine, a handsome buck, emerged from the forest to gaze upon the cabin and look for Peggy Heston, who befriends any animal that wanders into her yard. Goldfine is back for his fifth year. He has one deformed antler, making this year's rack identical to last year's set.

When he arrived, he chased the feeding does away and then, after establishing his dominance, stood back absolutely

motionless for a few minutes and let them eat. Remaining motionless is a protective maneuver.

Three bucks, three does and a fawn have been coming in the morning and evening to feed.

A young lady wood duck has been a guest for two months, and although her reaction to corn has been one of distaste, she makes a three-times-daily trip to join the 150 mallards that flock to the grounds. She is small and gets little consideration from her green-headed friends, who often step on her indiscriminately. Sometimes she waits at the back door until Peg comes out to escort her personally back to the lake.

On one duck-feeding occasion a buck that had come down to eat was confronted with this seemingly endless string of ducks that waddled from the water to turn the ground into a squirming mass of webbed feet and feathers. He was so entranced that he forgot to eat.

One blackduck that was banded seven years ago and one mallard are the only two banded birds in the flock. The children and grandchildren of the original birds, which were introduced to the Trail by Don Lobdell of Rockwood Lodge, have returned to nest every year.

A robin has defied the signs of a late fall and calls each morning from a nearby limb.

A gull, dubbed Henrietta, comes when called. This is the bird who was given first aid when it arrived with an injured eye. [1971]

GUNFLINT TRAIL UPGRADE. New construction has started on the upper end of the Gunflint Trail a mile south of the Sea Gull Lake public landing and extending toward the Sea Gull Guard Station. Work for the next ten weeks will be concentrated on cutting off curves and filling in the swampy areas.

The Gunflint Trail is classified as a Federal Forest Highway. The activity along the Gunflint, as we know it today, started from 1915 to 1925. The original logging road had become an access road for tourists, and small resorts were springing up.

Since then the Trail has been improved primarily with federal funds and is built according to federal specifications and at the whim of the government. These federal funds are apportioned to various road projects throughout the state. It is only the drippings from time to time that come to our county. Perhaps that is why it has taken forty-odd years to widen, gravel and partially blacktop the 60 miles length of the Gunflint Trail.

As the wheels of government slowly grind away give it another 10 years and the Trail will no doubt be blacktopped clear to the end. At that time the powers that be may find the portion that was first paved is fast wearing out. [1975]

The tree-clearing operation on the two and a half miles of road reconstruction beyond the Sea Gull Guard Station is an example of the rapid change in logging techniques that we have seen in the past few years.

I was told that with the sophisticated equipment now employed the entire operation can be done by three men who know their business and handle their machines with deft skill. Seeing is believing, so I had to have a look.

One machine, the cutter, is a small tracked contraption with a pair of cutter blades and two arms. The machine is maneuvered up to a tree with the open cutter just off the ground. The arms are extended around the tree, six feet up in a bear hug. Pressure is applied on the blades, the tree is severed and the operator backs the machine away from the cut and carries the tree up to a loading area. The tree is then tipped backward and forward like a whip in slow motion and is plopped down on an ever-growing tree pile. The machine literally walks through the forest snipping one tree after the next.

A big four-wheel tree farmer, which travels the terrain as if it had separate joints, with each wheel doing its thing, is backed up to a pile of trees. A clamp is lowered, a pile of neatly stacked trees is grabbed and the machine drags the load to another piece of equipment parked alongside the road. The trees, one at a time, are then picked up with a clamp and dropped onto an apparatus that shoves the log into the machine, where the tree is cut into eight-foot lengths and rolled out onto the side arms. As the log is fed in for each successive cut two knives advance along the tree, severing all the limbs. The clamp swings around, picks up the bundle of logs that has accumulated on the two side arms and neatly pivots it onto a pile ready for hauling.

Nothing is left but a small cluster of limbs and treetops, which are burned. The operation is known as clear-cutting, and that it is.

PARTRIDGE HUNTING.   The partridge season has started and will be open for several months.

I watched a couple of people the other day as they slowly drove along the road looking for partridge. They spotted one just ahead of the car and pulled to one side. The bird was pecking gravel, unconcerned with any activity nearby.

The driver quietly opened the front door, ducked down to remain unseen, and then opened the back door and worked his gun out of the case. He placed his gun over the hinge of the open front door and took careful aim as the bird continued to eat. There was a silent click, for no shell was in the chamber.

He quickly recocked his gun and shot. The partridge fluttered its last flip, and a little dog jumped out of the car and ran to hold the bird down for its master.

Although many of us hunt in the same manner, I sometimes wonder what instinct motivates us to carry out the act. In most instances it is not for food nor the excitement of seeing a bird drop in mid-flight. I wonder why we wouldn't feel the same excitement if we walked into a yard with chickens picking at the gravel and shot one. [1975]

Some years back before the enactment of restraining laws, the grouse were killed by the hundreds. In late August and September the broods keep close company and thus entire coveys can be eliminated. The final destruction of these birds was avoided by establishing seasons and bag limits.

The spruce grouse, near extinction and completely protected just a few years ago, is again endangered. Experience seems to be little heeded. Year after year partridge seasons are extended, and the grouse supply is ever dwindling.

DON BRAZELL. For 10 years Don Brazell had a long but determined struggle with cancer.

During most of his working career, he was part of the Gunflint Trail and its people. His work on the Trail started with a weekly beer and trucking service, but he did a multitude of errands and picked up our mail as a courtesy.

During World War II, with gas and food rationing, we would all have been left out on a thin, brittle limb if Don hadn't acquired two passenger buses. After much negotiating with the state Railroad and Warehouse Commission, he acquired the right to pick up incoming guests in Duluth and deliver them to their various destinations along the Gunflint Trail. His service was called The Wilderness Express.

His beer and trucking service went to all the lodges. Later a three-times-a-week mail service was initiated. Before that we relied on our old-time guests to pick up our mail in Grand Marais before coming to the lodge. Finally, the mail service grew and became a daily feature that extended from early spring to late fall. During good weather and bad, Don's arrival time seldom varied.

Then bone cancer appeared, and the long struggle began. There were times when he gained and times when he lost, but he kept up an eternal fight to live and again become active. His love for the Trail and its people never faltered.

In his last hours when Don was hurting mightily, he still whispered to me, "It is always good to see someone from the Trail." [1980]

THE CHINA SYNDROME. One day Jane and Gene Gasper glanced across the lake toward Gunflint Lodge, and saw heavy smoke. Jane called Nancy Thompson, who thought Gunflint Lodge might be burning brush.

At almost the same instant, Sue Kerfoot here at Gunflint wandered up to the outfitter's complex and discovered that the sauna building was on fire. The building contained not only the sauna and dressing rooms, but also a series of showers and bathroom fixtures in storage.

By this time the building was burning lustily, and all efforts were concentrated on saving the nearby dormitories. Jewel Stephan, who was working at Gunflint Lodge, made calls in rapid succession, and people came from everywhere.

Jim and Eric Thompson from Borderland with pump and hose, the Gaspers, Ken Desch, Chuck Gecas from Heston's, Bob Cushman from Sea Gull, Carl Higgins from Saganaga, Don Enzenauer from Sea Gull River, the Leeds from Tuscarora and Carl Brandt from Poplar Lake were among the volunteers. Finally the government firefighters arrived with a more powerful pump to attach to Gunflint's hose.

Although in her calls Jewel asked for available men, she missed a bet, for Pip, Debbie and Marie Mark are all equally capable of throwing a pump and hose on a truck, setting it up and operating it where needed. They called back to inform Jewel of their availability. Most men and women on the Trail can handle such situations with equal ability.

The thing that really counted was the presence of fire

133

GUNFLINT

pumps and hoses cached at key resort locations and the speed with which the volunteers came to take their places.

The emergency ended when the unpredictable and gusty wind suddenly stopped. Soon the fire was out, and all was calm.

An interesting side note: Where once there were iron tubs and metal shower stalls, we now use a plastic enclosure. It melts beautifully to a final blob of ash. [1980]

IT'S A BIRD, IT'S A. . . . A couple staying at Heston's Lodge saw a large bird swimming on the far side of the lake. They had no binoculars, so the man stepped to the shore to have a better look. He decided it was a loon, the biggest he had ever seen. He called to his wife to have a look at the big bird swimming in his direction.

It seemed to be swimming with wings outstretched until suddenly two ears came into focus. The large bird was transformed into a moose. It headed straight for Virl Vogan's dock.

As all this was happening Virl was unloading a new television set, with Greg Gecas helping him. They started down their path, one on each side of the bulky burden, when they were confronted by the moose. Having arrived on the shore, it was making its way up the same trail.

There was a face-to-face confrontation. Virl didn't know whether to drop the TV set or stand his ground.

The moose solved the problem by stepping to one side and climbing onto the main road, only to encounter an oncoming car. He dashed back, missing Greg and Virl by a small margin.

Then, taking refuge behind a small shed and peeking around the corner cautiously, it remained immobile and half hidden for several minutes.

Virl hurried to the house for his camera. No film. The moose sauntered off. [1982]

HEDSTROM'S MILL. At Clearwater Lodge Wes Hedstrom showed a short movie taken years ago by Dr. William Bagley of Duluth.

Dr. Bagley had at one time visited the Hedstrom sawmill for a couple of weeks during the time it was located on Sucker Lake, which is now renamed Moon Lake, north of East Bearskin.

About a hundred people came to Clearwater Lodge to catch a glimpse of the history of the logging company that the Hedstroms started 75 years ago.

The sawmills were actually portable units that were relocated every two or three years. Their main activity was centered around East Bearskin, Caribou, Alder and south of Poplar Lake.

In the 1940s and '50s the chain saw was introduced. It was so heavy it took two people to operate. In a few years it was improved and could be handled by one person.

It was during this period that the Hedstrom mill reached a high yearly production of half-a-million board feet. The camps were self-sustaining with 300 men on the payroll. It was a time when eight hours was just a warmup for the twelve-hour work day.

In 1948 the mobile camp became permanently located at the site of the present planing mill north of Grand Marais on Maple Hill. A band saw was installed in 1975. It was thought the ultimate mechanical development had been reached.

Following the fire of 1984, some new computer-controlled equipment was installed. Now Hedstroms are producing 10 million board feet a year and have a capacity of producing 14 million board feet. [1985]

A DAY ON THE WATER. The day was overcast and we were enjoying one of those rare occasions when the waters remain dead calm except for the intermittent sigh by a wind that only ruffles the surface and passes on. A gentle mist occasionally was brightened by a peek-through of the sun. Reflections appeared and faded like a will-o'-the-wisp.

We were on a one-day canoe trip, complete with portages and gentle rapids.

From a secluded bay a blue heron rose with its wide majestic wings, lifting its stork-like body over the tree tops and vanishing. They are wary birds and resent intrusions.

A kingfisher hurried to a high limb overhanging the water where it could look for a meal and make a quick plunge to sweep up an unsuspecting victim.

I cast with an Ugly Bug over the top of a weed bed, and a quick skittering retrieve enticed a bass to strike and rise out of the water in tail-spinning leaps. A bare rock served as a lunch site.

Hidden beneath a screen of trees were purple asters and clumps of straw flowers denoting the approach of fall. An occasional fisherman glided by silently, purposefully going ever farther to catch that big one.

On a few lakes where beaver had once controlled the water level and have since been trapped out, the damp receding shoreline was rich with patches of red water smartweed.

A half dozen blackducks paddled by, unafraid. Obviously they had been tossed a tidbit now and then by a passing canoeist.

A worm attached to a weighted bait that slithered across the uneven lake bottom produced a walleye from time to time. A loon called plaintively across the water. Soon the loons will be off on their flight south.

As the afternoon waned canoe parties staked out their campsites. The silence we had enjoyed this day was broken by the arrival of a group who washed and banged pots amidst shouts and gales of laughter. They took a swim with flops and splashes.

From far off, on the Canadian side of the border, we heard the zing of a chain saw and the grumblings of large logging

equipment as timber was dropped and hauled off to an ever-consuming market.

A butterfly hesitated for a moment's visit. Its wings and body were a soft velvety brown trimmed in yellow with an inner lining of blue dots.

A fuzzy caterpillar, yellow spotted and sprinkled with long white sensory hairs, inched its way across a rock, determined on some unknown destination. It crawled up on my finger. When I lifted it high in the air, the caterpillar extended itself from the sheer precipice into a space of nothingness. When there was no firm footing ahead, it backed up and shot into the air like an arrow released from a taut bow to land at my feet as gently as down. [1981]

BEAR TALES. Ed and Myrt Cavanaugh had a Chihuahua named Porky. Once when a large bear ambled toward their lodge, Porky gave chase and followed it to the top of a hill.

Ed, sensing danger, called to the dog. Porky stopped and turned at the call of his master, at which time the bear sneaked up, gave the dog a stunning swat and plunked his paw on the dog's chest. Ed tore to the rescue, shouting as he ran. The bear lifted his paw, freed Porky and strolled off into the woods.

On another occasion, when the mighty Porky was protecting his territory by chasing a bear, the bear suddenly stopped to see what was at its heels. Upon seeing this spindly mouse, the bear let out a snarl and with jaws wide open started in pursuit of the dog. The Chihuahua, after one glance down the bear's gullet, tore for home, rolling down the hill head over heels in its eagerness to reach safety. It scrambled under the building in time to see the frustrated bear walk by. [1963]

Electric light and telephone trouble developed at Gateway and Swanson's Lodge. The cause was inexplicable, with neither wind nor a storm to account for the sudden outage.

When the REA investigated, they discovered from tracks and claw marks that two bears had been fighting in the vicinity of the Hungry Jack Lake open dump. One bear chased the other up the electric pole. The bear on the pole became entangled in the wires and got a "hot shot." It dropped to the ground and, after pawing the ground in the vicinity of the pole, departed from the scene. The mystery was solved.

Eleven bears are hanging around the dump. One huge bear was estimated by Pat McDonnell to weigh from five hundred to six hundred pounds. Pat said he had to dump the garbage fast or the impatient bears would quickly move in to help with the unloading. In spite of all the warnings to guests of the area, one tourist was seen hand feeding potato chips to one of the bears.

At Borderland Lodge a bear entered the porch of one of the cabins, taking the screen with him. Finding nothing of interest to eat, he went through the screened porch of another cabin and sat on the table while the ladies were cooking fish in the kitchen.

One of the men in the party accosted the bear and hit it over the nose with a flashlight. This had little effect. It was really the screaming of the women and the general commotion that caused the bear to retreat. He hung around the back door of the lodge until 4:30 a.m., still hoping for a handout.

At Gunflint Lodge a bear walked into the dry storeroom, picked up a 50-pound sack of flour and walked out. He clasped the paper-covered sack in his front paws and walked upright in a swaying motion. He shifted his weight from one hind leg to the other. The sack tore open, leaving a zigzag trail of flour through the woods, ending with an empty sack torn to shreds. What a frustrated bear he was when he discovered his filching had gained him nothing.

NORTHWOODS PERSPECTIVES. The dawn haze rises slowly from the hollows like curling smoke, weaving itself into dreams and meditations. Silently, in the coming of day, a buck leads his doe and fawn along invisible highways through green timber. They stop, look about, twitch their ears, then follow down the trail.

Gradually the forest emerges from the gray pallor to a light and rich green splendor. The sun lifts over the hill, and all is bathed in a morning light. The lake beckons with a long silvery finger, and we respond with the thrill of a gliding canoe to the lure of the wilderness.

Clouds scud high overhead but are met by an unseen weather force and stop. Silence envelops the forest. The birds are no longer sing. The water remains still. Creatures peer anxiously in all directions. The leaves hang motionless, and the loons have ceased their calling. The air is trapped, as if in the ominous tranquility of the eye of a hurricane. A leaf flutters.

The wind rises, whitecaps build and vie with each other to reach even greater heights. A black cloud approaches. Lightning begins to dart to unpredictable landing points while thunder peals in earth-rattling force. We are placed in proper perspective.

Our self-established importance is nil. Our accomplishments, which may have a momentary value, are quickly erased and forgotten. We are humbled. We see that we are but a speck of the infinite matter that comprises the universe. May we always see things as they are. [1980]

OCTOBER

First Snow

EARLY IN THIS MONTH the coloring of the forest reaches its peak. Golden leaves of the trembling aspen dance in the slightest breeze. Next the leaves will lose their hold on their host trees and fall, brown and spent, to join their companions on the ground.

Flocks of geese hasten across the sky in groups of six to almost a hundred. Once I saw a large flock emerge from behind a mist-covered hill with its leadership in question. The geese bunched and spread and bunched again. After much argument and discussion a leader took charge of the flight The birds gathered into their formation and headed south.

LOST RESORTS. Ashes to ashes and dust to dust. We held a wake when End of the Trail Lodge closed its doors for the last time. End of the Trail Lodge was started in 1931 by Russell and Eve Blankenburg and was called Saganaga Fishing Camp. The log dining room and lounge was built by Harry Hummich, a perfectionist with an ax.

In 1946 Al and Mary Hedstrom purchased the resort and changed the name to End of the Trail. Al promoted the lodge and the lake intensely and established the reputation of Saganaga as an outstanding walleye lake. As an American Plan resort they carried on a successful business. Due to an illness they were forced to sell the resort. Its last owners were Nick and Mary Beth Helm.

End of the Trail Lodge had a number of guests who brought their own boats and motors—many of them over 25 horsepower. The new BWCA regulations that limited the motor size to 25-horse on the U.S. side of Saganaga discouraged a sizable portion of the clientele, who then chose to go elsewhere. On the Canadian side of the lake there was no horsepower limitation.

End of the Trail had been a bustling and busy resort that employed many guides and a large staff. Other resorts also have been caught in the vortex of new BWCA restrictions and subsequently swept to oblivion. The owners of Chik-Wauk Lodge, Saganaga Outfitters, Zopff's Outfitters, Douglas' Outfitters, and Sea Gull Lodge and Outfitters chose to sell to the government. The loss of these businesses and the money they generated in the county threw an additional tax load on the remaining property owners. [1979]

CANOE TRIPPERS, BEWARE. About 30 years ago a group of fellows, some of them guides at Gateway Lodge, decided to take a late fall canoe trip. Bob Zimmerman, Fred Brouillette, Loren Leng and Ralph Jackson made up the party.

It just so happened that several girls were on a canoe trip at the same time in the same area. Ellen Bedell, Polly Miles and Dorothy McQuire were in this group. Of course it was quite by chance that the two groups met.

A few years later Bob Zimmerman and Ellen Bedell, and Fred Brouillette and Polly Miles, were united in marriage. Recently the two couples joined once more to celebrate their 25th wedding anniversary at Gateway Lodge.

It was a gala affair. Fifty-five guests from Duluth, Minneapolis, Iowa and Grand Marais joined in the dinner-party celebration.

The McDonnells of Gateway Lodge had prepared a feast to be long remembered. Bette McDonnell prepared an assortment of 25 hors d'oeuvres, which were served at the cocktail hour, followed by a full-course chicken dinner.

A local group played music for the evening dancing, with the *schottische* a frequent favorite. The lodge walls reverberated with joy and happiness.

Among those present were Bob Zimmerman's mother and other members of his immediate family, and six former guides of Gateway, who recalled some of their experiences and escapades of that time. Sammy Zimmerman, also there, reminisced about early days of the Trail. If his stories had been recorded, what an insight into those times we would have. [1959]

OUR SCHOOL BUS. In 1958 we didn't have a daily school bus during the entire school year, only during the fall closing and spring opening of our resorts. The only options we year-round residents had were to board the children with some family in Grand Marais, move to Grand Marais or teach the

143

children at home. Personally we used all three options at different times over the years.

On one October morning in 1958 the school bus was to make its last fall run. Bud Kratoska, the driver, started off on schedule from his home at 5:30 a.m.

At 6:30 the Trail youngsters were waiting dutifully at their side road pickup spots. After a rather long wait Al Hedstrom from the End of the Trail collected a load of children and headed down the Trail to meet Bud.

He hadn't found him by the time he reached Rockwood, so he stopped and called Grand Marais. No one knew of the whereabouts of the missing bus and driver. Al continued toward town while Charlet Kratoska started coming up the Trail. In between them sat a dejected Bud with two flat tires and one spare.

GEESE AND SNOW.   A large flock of snow geese settled for a moment on Gunflint Lake, seemingly to discuss further flight plans.

The next day at about dusk Pat McDonnell and Billy Needham watched a flight of what they estimated to be 600 to 800 geese in four separate V formations circle as if to land on Hungry Jack Lake but then adjust their flight pattern and continue on west.

A couple of days later, just before a windy, gusty rainstorm usurped a sunny sky, Alice Brandt on Poplar Lake watched a flight of about a hundred birds traveling in cadence to the west. So batten down the hatches, folks—our fall honeymoon may be drawing to a speedy close. We believe the adage that says snow will follow geese. [1962]

With the exception of a golden crown worn here and there by a birch matriarch, the deciduous trees stand stripped and bare, waiting to be bedecked with snow. The fallen leaves add a pungent odor as I tread the freshly carpeted path.

GROUSE AND SNOW. It was the opening weekend of partridge season and most everyone had shot their limit of birds. Then the snows came. A sticky, gooey mess a foot deep left innumerable cars stranded like flies in freshly poured honey.

As so often happens during strong winds and swirling snow it seems to become imperative for people to move. Without snow tires or chains, vehicles were useless. Cars collected one after the other at the base of Gunflint Hill, and their occupants came trudging to Gunflint Lodge for food and shelter.

Many summer-home people who were up for partridge season became unscheduled and stranded guests at Gateway Lodge. Bearskin Lodge became a refuge, too, as did Trail Service Center.

The wind roared and toppled trees which knocked out the power and telephone lines. The Arrowhead Electric crew struggled in the dark and the swirling snow to restore order.

Walt Bunn on Hungry Jack Lake dispensed chains, which he sent by boat from one summer-home owner to the other. The chains came back torn. Links had to be replaced. The hammer in the garage made a rat-a-tat-tat sound in defiance of the elements.

The snowplow made a night run, and by morning the cars were freed and struggling to reach the snow-free strip. If nature follows its usual routine it will be but a few days before the ground will be bare again. [1965]

MORE THAN ONE WAY TO GET A GROUSE. During the hunting season guns are the usual weapons, but other methods are tried, too. Take Bud Bent for instance. He had a truck with a part missing from the grill. Driving along the road, he noticed a large owl that tried to lift off the road but seemed tied or weighted down. A collision was inevitable, but the result was ludicrous.

The owl had a partridge in its talons that it refused to release and whose weight had kept it from rising. When the bird and truck collided, it was the hole in the grill in which the birds landed. The partridge fell out. Bud went back and picked it up. It was completely defeathered and had one tear on its breast. The owl fell out of the hole in the grill, picked itself up, shook and flew off.

Over at Caribou Lake, at Ernie Simon's house, when the wind was ripping and snorting across the lake a partridge came through a double-glass window, shattering the first and leaving a neat round bird-size hole in the second glass.

After a few moments, stunned from the impact, the bird picked itself up from the shattered glass and started to peck at the design in the rug. The resident youngsters decided it needed its freedom and turned it loose.

THE GUNFLINT OPEN. Ralph Griffis of Chik-Wauk Lodge had a bucket of 70 floater golf balls outside his office door. They were for guests to practice a shot now and then. They could tee off and drive toward a target in the bay.

The season having tapered off, Ralph decided to take a few shots himself to get into form for a round of golf at some future time this winter. He took a golf club from the bag and reached for a ball in the bucket. It was completely empty. Who had swiped all the balls?

He searched through his mind for the people who had been into his place the past few days and came to the conclusion that no one who had stopped by would commit this act. Friends suggested one animal or another as the culprit.

To test their theories Ralph dropped into the bucket a few beat-up golf balls. Next morning, the balls were gone. He added six more. Next morning, same result.

The challenge had to be met. Ralph decided he would sit up for a night and watch the bucket to catch who was doing the stealing and find out where he might go to retrieve his 70 floater golf balls—and by this time almost 20 regular golf balls. He took up his vigil in a chair before the window, but dozed from time to time. At about three o'clock he was awakened by a rustling and beheld a fox, who reached into the pail, took a ball and scurried off.

Great! The mystery would soon be solved and the balls recovered. In a short time the fox was back, but this time took two balls in another direction. The puzzle became more confusing. Again the fox returned and took the last two balls and trotted off in a third direction. The fox still had the upper hand, for now cached in various and sundry areas were 90 balls.

A few nights later it snowed. It was just what Ralph had been waiting for. With sublime confidence he placed 20 beat-up golf balls in the pail by the door. Now at long last he would be able to recover the hundred balls that had been buried in the nearby woods by the sneaky fox.

In the morning he hurried to the pail—18 balls were gone and two remained. The snow did not reveal neat paths leading to a single hiding place but rather a maze of tracks going in every direction. It looked as if a hundred foxes had joined in a rendezvous.

Ralph hunted and hunted to no avail, but in the midst of his intense search he heard a sound. Out in the road was the red fox rolling on his back in the snow. His mouth was wide open in a big grin. At last report the fox had not as yet carted off the golf clubs. [1966]

HIKING THE ESKER. An esker stretches across a section of Cook Country near us. When this land was covered by a glacier, a subterranean river flowed through a deep crevasse carrying sand, gravel and rocks. As the ice melted the river bed, 30 to 60 feet thick in most places, was left like a meandering ridge. Years ago from the air it looked like an imposing crooked wall. Now it has been overgrown with brush and trees and is not as discernible.

From the Gunflint Trail just below the Mink Lake road, on a curve a road leads to a gravel pit. Actually the pit is part of the old esker and this site has always been a handy place to obtain gravel.

Two of us hiked to the top of the esker where we could get a view for miles around. Farther in we came upon a wide creek that defied crossing. We sat a few moments to rest. There we saw two beavers swimming silently in narrowing arcs.

One beaver directly in front of us grabbed a long narrow stick in its front paws and methodically nibbled the bark, leaving the stick completely bare. The animal looked like a flute player. The only discernible sound was the murmur of its mate. As the flute player munched on the stick the second beaver swam close to touch its nose and then swam off about its business.

We watched until the stick was thoroughly cleaned. The beaver looked it over carefully, trimmed a stub, determined the food was gone and threw it aside. [1966]

PORKIES. A little over a half century ago when I first came here there was an abundance of porcupine. The porcupine were protected, for that was the one animal that could easily be killed with a club and thus assure a meal to anyone who became lost.

Their numbers continued to be high through the dog team days. I spent a lot of time pulling quills from my dogs that had challenged this creature.

For generations the porkies were the source of quills for the Indians to decorate their birch-bark baskets. And then suddenly the porcupines were gone.

Many things could have brought about the change: disease, lack of available food, or an over-abundance of fisher.

Fisher were adept at attacking the vulnerable, unquilled underside of the porcupine.

Last week, high in an aspen, a porcupine sat and watched traffic roll along the Trail. A conflict may arise between U.S. Forest Service tree-planting projects and this bark-feeding animal. [1980]

SCAVENGERS. Ravens are great scavengers. For a few days a young bear that had been killed and left in the ditch near the Mayhew Lake road served as a succulent meal for the ravens. They attacked the belly first and then the rib cage, where the feasting was really good.

Ravens are wary and fly off when approached. If you stand semi-hidden near a kill hoping for a picture of the ravens feeding you usually will be found by a spotter raven who flies overhead. The spotter will give a series of warning calls for the flock to stay away. If a car whizzes by the birds will rise, leave momentarily and then quickly return.

In this case, after a few days the bear was removed from the roadside and the feast ended.

A skunk was hit near Cross River, and the ravens moved in again. I wonder if these bold birds acquired a skunky halitosis. [1982]

UP PERISCOPE. A few days ago while paddling on a small lake, I encountered a group of five otters. As they became aware of my presence they rose up in the water. Their heads protruded like periscopes, high and straight for better vision. They didn't like my canoe advancing on them, so they scurried toward a group of large boulders at the water's edge. Here they were completely hidden and secure. As I paddled by their refuge they expressed their opinion of the intrusion by hissing.

The female otter can breed at two years old. The young stay with the mother for most of the first year. The male does not breed successfully until he is six or seven years old. [1985]

LOONS AND WEATHER. I received a note from Irv Benson of Saganaga stating that he missed the weather forecasting that he had gained from the loons since their departure south.

When I asked for enlightenment I received the following answer:

The first year I worked for Al Hedstrom at End of the Trail Lodge I started guiding fishermen. I had some fellows who wanted to fish for lake trout on Saganaga west of American Point. Tempest Powell was also guiding for Al at the time and made the not-too-difficult observation that one certain person planning to go west on Sag that day needed some experience and advised me not to go down there with the boat, motor and gear we used back then, as I'd probably spend the day windbound.

Being about as receptive to local advice as a first-time camper or fisherman in this area, and as dense as a granite boulder, I charged out past the lighthouse with the two fellows and gathered them in the usual Shell Lake wooden boat with its mighty 5-horse Johnson.

Having more curiosity than sense, I did ask how the heck Tempest knew I was due to be wind-bound out there when I hadn't even started yet. It was glassy smooth on every bit of the water I could see from the dock.

Tempest said the loons were flying and hollering earlier that morning when he got up. So, thinking what the loons did was strictly their affair, and also prodded a bit by Al to proceed promptly with the business of lending some credence to his advertising literature, I cranked up the mighty 5-horse Johnson and off we went. Had I looked back I probably would have seen Tempest shaking her head.

I never made it for supper. Tempest did, for she took her party east on Sag to some ridiculously safe place that I've long forgotten the name of, probably Gapens Bay or Northern Light Rapids. I think Rolf Skrien was also guiding that day, and although I am not sure of it, he no doubt went to Sag Falls with his people. He had a year more experience than myself, and considerable better sense.

It seems that loons have a sort of built-in weather sensor someplace within their fuselage. We believe that 8 to 12 hours before a high wind or bad storm, they spend a lot of their time flying around shrieking out the word. Invariably they're right. Even up to a day after this noise, the local area experiences a high wind, a bad storm or some other form of terribleness to anyone out on the lake with a boat or canoe. This seems to hold true throughout the midsummer months. It is occasionally erroneous in the early spring and again in the late fall. [1985]

A VISITOR. A weasel took up residence in the Bruce and Sue Kerfoot home. The weasel was in the transition state, half brown and half white. Although the weasel is an excellent mouser Sue did not enjoy seeing a slick little body suddenly appear from a nook or cranny—to vanish and reappear around another corner.

A window was left open during the evening to encourage its escape. In the middle of the night Sue heard a great rustle of papers in the office. She prodded Bruce out of bed to investigate the night marauder. The weasel had obligingly gone out the window, but a flying squirrel had swooped in as a replacement. [1972]

BATS. We have had a preview of Halloween. There has been a surge of bats that flit back and forth on many of the side roads. They appear in the afternoons as well as in the evenings. The warm weather that has produced a new crop of bugs may be the beckoning force.

The arrival of the bats led to a discovery, for me at least.

Normally when a bat inadvertently gets inside the house, my method of pest control has been to use a fish net. I have climbed on chairs and couches, often making a vain sweep as the black creature swooped by. In my pursuit I have bumped pictures and tripped over lamps.

The other evening I propped open the door to enjoy a waft of fresh air. Four bats promptly flew into the house. I thought that if a light brought them in, maybe a light would take them out. I turned off the house lights, turned on the outside light and kept the door open. Lo and behold, they promptly departed into the night. [1974]

MILLION-DOLLAR QUESTION. With all the changes in the forest and its uses how does one push time back 60 or 70 years and reproduce the forest of that time? This question comes to mind as I consider the proposal of the Safari Gun Club, backed by the Sierra Club, to introduce a herd of caribou on Little Saganaga.

That location has been chosen because there is caribou moss on the islands, and because there are few wolves in the area. I suppose the caribou, during their penned rehabilitation period, will be taught that they cannot swim from island to mainland.

From what I gather in the write-up in the Sierra Club Bulletin, the proponents of the plan are thrilled with the anticipation of sitting by a campfire on Little Saganaga and looking up to see a caribou gazing at them from the other side of the flickering flames (now restricted to a cooking fire within Forest Service grates). According to a game warden this may never transpire, because the campsites on these newly stocked islands may be closed.

More pertinent to the issue and the proposal to spend a million dollars is this question: Why should it be necessary to introduce caribou when moose and deer prevail naturally now? [1978]

BEAR TALES. The berries are gone, the leaves have fallen and the bears are making their last sortie to add a layer of fat to sustain them through the winter.

It is interesting to note that black bears once lived throughout most of North America. Now, due in part to a change of habitat, they are no longer found in many of their former sites.

In Minnesota the bears are largely restricted to the northeastern portion of the state. The bears have learned in recent years that easy pickings come from garbage dumps and campsites. [1983]

The bear that had been roaming among the homes on Gunflint Lake before hibernation scented an enticing aroma at Borderland Lodge. A man and his son, occupying an upstairs villa, had brewed a tasty stew for a late dinner. With the sliding glass door left ajar the odor had spread outdoors.

Soon after retiring, Nancy Thompson heard a heavy tread along the upstairs balcony. She poked Jim, who had just dropped into that first blissful sleep, to inform him of her hunch. He drowsily muttered it couldn't be and prepared to settle back into oblivion. Another hard jab. With an "oh well," he grabbed a flashlight to have a look and pacify his spouse.

As he rounded the corner he met the bear walking casually down the steps. The bear had gone upstairs, stood upright with his paws on the screen door and surveyed the situation. The presence of people discouraged further investigation.

The next bear stop was Gunflint Lodge, where a freezer stood in an anteway. Sundry articles were piled on the lid. With one swish of a bear paw all of the objects were pushed to the floor and the lid raised. The bear crawled into the box and consumed a prime rib roast, leaving one tiny bone as a token. [1979]

The time came when new regulations were initiated, a season established and bears shot for sport. The sport consisted in hanging out some rotten meat, sitting off to one side and waiting until a bear came to feed.

Tumsey Johnson discovered, on a late trip to Saganaga, that bears had ransacked 14 or 15 cabins on the northeast arm of the lake. Elinor's cabin as well as Mike Deschampe's, Jack Powell's and the Old Trading Post had all been entered and vandalized.

Tumsey figured it could not be the work of one bear. It seemed to be an entire platoon that hiked and swam its way from cabin to cabin. Although their reward was not great, invariably they broke in the front door, tore things apart and departed through a window. When encountering a tent bears go in the front and rip a hole in the side or back to make their exit. It will soon be hibernation time. Cheers!

FAREWELL TO FALL. The ground is sprinkled with snow. Ducks circle uneasily in large groups or wing their way in pairs, slowly building the necessary strength for their fall migration. The sky presents gray layers, which occasionally separate and make room for the slanted rays of the sun. The greens and yellows of the far hills wave back and forth like fans.

This fall the monsoon rains have filled the creeks and swamps with a bonus of water. The winds have whipped the lakes into frothy, seething, churning waves.

Soon a blanket of snow will turn our country into a contrast of blacks and whites. It will be the time for snowshoes or skis, the putt of a snowmobile or the yipping of a straining dog team.

Fall is not waning. It is gone. [1964]

NOVEMBER

Time To Be Wary

EVERYTHING IN THIS COUNTRY is on a grand scale. Take variations in the weather, for example. We have wild swings. One year is mild, another severe. One year we have an abundance of rain, the next is dry and we're vulnerable to fires. We might have a year of snows waist deep or a pittance barely up to our knees.

Even during a single season we can have dramatic contrasts. But whatever the weather, we will be wary.

It has occurred to me in some years that summer hasn't wiggled in between this winter and last but that winter has become one continuous season. This is an especially common thought when the temperature drops below zero for the first time.

Then on another day it turns mild. The trees shake their burden of snow and straighten with a swish. It rains, and the moisture-laden snow dissolves and vanishes. Rain patters on rooftops like tiny footsteps.

A thin glaze of ice had formed in the shallow fingerling bays of several lakes. Pushed by light winds, it breaks into pieces, creating tinkling metallic sounds like tiny cymbals as it disappears. The woods become wet and drippy like a huge rain forest.

OLD MAN'S BEARD. Along the wooded trail club mosses stand erect. Some of them extend their miniature golden candles skyward.

Common lichens like the green-lobed *tripe de roche* were boiled and eaten by explorers in times of extreme hunger. It is as inspiring to taste as I think a piece of boiled old shoe leather would be. This lichen lies flat on a rock with tight curled edges like foaming, capped breakers in a turbulent sea.

Other lichens are highly valued for the rich and varied color obtained from them. The Indians used them for dyes. The under portions of these plants that rest on moss have many cilia-like filaments that slowly dissolve the hardest rock with their seeping acids.

Old man's beard, a favorite food of the moose, hangs limply with lacy grace from dead limbs. On the ground clumps of gray caribou moss, individual stems resembling

many-branched antlers, look like a miniature prehistoric forest. The blankets of moss found on fallen dead and decaying tree trunks, on close examination, are seen to be thick feathery ferns and trumpet-like spore cases.

DEER HUNTING.   I find great reward in being in the woods at this time of year.

As I stand motionless a flock of chickadees alights in a tree overhead, flitting on ever-lower branches until one has a daring yen to land on my red topknot cap. A squirrel scurries down a tree and sticks half of its body into a deep hole, with just a rear haunch protruding. Quickly the squirrel retrieves its previously deposited cache. Its forepaws hold and turn the tidbits before nibbling the goodies.

A woodpecker flits to a nearby tree and whacks away for a morsel. Wisps of bearded moss stand out on birch bark like miniature truncated trees. In some areas thick sphagnum moss has laid a soft carpet for me. Leafless trees, bushes and cliffs stand out in their stark nakedness. Partridge silently appear on mincing feet.

As I move on I notice where an otter has left its tracks down a side hill where it slid for long stretches and took a few jumps, then slid again. It traveled across a frozen pond, running and bellyflopping.

On a hillside in a wind-blown area moss hangs from the branches. Deer have munched on this essential food item. A stream gurgles down the hillside and disappears in quiet pools under rocks and roots and then reappears.

But I'm hunting. I am reminded of that, and that it's deer season, when I hear a snort and catch a quick glimpse of a white flag and the bounding rear end of a deer as it makes a flying leap and then vanishes noiselessly.

High on top of a hill I come upon a fresh beaver cutting. There is no lake in the area, so I investigate. On the very edge of a swamp I find the neatest system of dams and terraces.

Above it all is a tiny pond with a huge beaver house. As I sit contemplating this marvel of engineering a large beaver quietly swims from the house and over to within a few feet of me. Satisfied that I am of no consequence, it examines the dam and swims quietly back to its house.

As I turn to go a fisher dashes across an open grassy spot. I see another buck, but he looks rangy and tough without much meat. Upon closer scrutiny it proves to be Russell Blankenburg from Sea Gull Lodge. I let him slip by.

As I follow the trail of a deer's meanderings I wonder why they walk where they walk—over a windfall, under tag alder, through the edge of thick balsam that reaches out and shakes a blob of snow down my neck. The deer roam up steep hills and down into gullies and are only momentarily discernible through small openings. They meander through sunny glades that sparkle and glisten and squeak with the gentle swaying of the tall pines.

As dots of red and orange bob around the woods I am aware of the many hunters. Few of them ever wander more than a quarter-mile from the road.

On Hungry Jack Lake a group of summer residents will be positioned at promising locations. Bob Zimmerman, a guide, aided by Walt Bunn, will beat the brush and diligently try to drive a deer by a specific point so one of these hunters can get a shot.

What is more apt to happen is that when Bob drives a deer past a stand or designated spot, he finds that the person who was assigned to this location has wandered off. The most likely place to find him will be back in Mother Bunn's kitchen sipping a cup of coffee.

Also in the woods are the stump sitters who alert deer by pulling out a pipe or a cigarette and lighting up for a smoke; and the restless hunters constantly on the move—breaking

twigs, rustling through dry leaves, stirring up chattering squirrels, climbing over rocks and in general letting everyone in the woods know of their presence.

PREDATORS. People seem so illogical. On the one hand, efforts are made by individuals and sportsmen's clubs to feed deer in the winter. At other times of the year hunters attempt to kill the deer, more often for sport than for food.

I often ask: Should people kill the wolf, who kills deer for food, just so that people may kill more deer for sport? Will the deer herd survive under the two devastating predators, people and wolves?

We had a large deer herd in the late 1960s and '70s. Their trails were heavily traveled. The season was open for about 10 days every other year. With the kills by the hunters and the kills by the wolves, the deer population seemed to stay in balance.

The old system was discarded and a new system introduced. It was said that the deer would soon starve for lack of food and that the deer season should be open every year. Slowly the herd grew smaller. It was said that wolves were to blame.

Wolves, both the timber wolf and the brush wolf (more recently identified as a coyote), were trapped and a bounty paid on them. They were hunted by planes and shot from the air as they sunned on the lakes. After two years of this the wolves who remained got wise, and at the sound of a plane they dashed for the timbered shore.

With the continued hunting pressure and shrinking of the herd, a no-fawn regulation was imposed. After a couple of years this was dropped, for who could tell when a fawn was a fawn? Too often the deer in the brush that seemed to have spikes turned out to be just a fawn. So the fawns that had been shot in error were left for the foxes and wolves to feast on. In 1988 all antlerless deer were protected.

The resorts had stopped taking hunters by this time. The deer had become so few that the trails in the woods showed signs of only an occasional deer or no deer at all.

With the virtual elimination of the deer the Department of Natural Resources decided to manage the area primarily for moose. With the thinning of the beaver ranks, wolf food became almost nonexistent, so the wolves moved on to more promising feeding grounds.

Suddenly there were few timber wolves, and they became an endangered species. No more wolf bounties, no more wolf trapping. After a couple of years this was changed to apply to timber wolves only. Brush wolves could still be trapped. The same trap is used for both species.

END OF A BEAVER COLONY. In late 1981 a complaint was made to the state Department of Natural Resources that beavers were cutting trees on private property. Game warden Bill Zickrick was authorized to issue a special permit and have the beavers trapped out.

Thus the pond at the west end of Gunflint Lake that had been in existence since the beginning of time lost its inhabitants—seven beavers. The dam was broken down and the pond water level lowered.

When people and animals collide head on, the animals are the losers. But people lose something too. How surprised the blue heron, ducks and marsh birds will be when they come back to their favorite nesting place and find it destroyed. How much the people nearby will miss those birds, who will go somewhere else to feed and raise their broods.

A member of that family of beavers was featured feasting on some green twigs in the television show *The Lady of the Gunflint.*

The beaver has been heavily trapped over the years. In many areas over-trapping has resulted in abandoned beaver

houses. This in turn often leads to broken-down beaver dams and a change of water levels in rivers and small lakes.

The extent of beaver trapping depends on the price of fur and the length of the open season. With the trapping that goes on now, the houses are invariably trapped clean.

The beaver colony is a family setup. Under normal conditions, young males are eventually driven out by the older adults. This usually happens when the young males are approaching two years of age. The mother, the oldest female of the colony, is making preparations for a new litter of young who are born in April, May and sometimes late in March.

Leaving the lodge where they were born, the two-year-old males strike out on their own, searching for mates and new areas for starting colonies. The yearlings remain in the old colony, but both they and their father move out of the main lodge before the young are born. For several months they live in temporary quarters nearby, leaving the old female and her babies in sole possession of the main lodge. Any bona fide trapper knows these facts.

In the 1940s and '50s, and even before that, a smattering of resort operators had established areas where they trapped to supplement their incomes. For the most part trapping was done in moderation to maintain a sustained yield. Each area was respected and not infringed upon by others.

The Minnesota Game and Fish Department (now called the Department of Natural Resources) had established a limit on the number of beaver that could be taken. Game and trapping regulations were vigorously enforced by the four or five game wardens who checked the traplines and back-woods trails.

The picture suddenly changed when a office was established for the Department of Natural Resources in Grand Marais. All areas were opened for anyone to trap. Beaver seasons were opened in the fall and also in the spring, when the females were having their young and were easy to trap. If one trapper didn't take all the beaver in a house, the next person would.

Camping in the woods and maintaining a trapline was replaced by road trapping. At one time the Trail had traps under every culvert and along all the ponds and streams that are available within easy reach of some road. Close to a thousand traps lined the Trail from one end to the other. Only two game wardens were on duty to enforce the rules. Their combined area included a thousand square miles of lands and waters.

At one time winter was the only beaver season. Trapping was more difficult then so only a few animals from each house were taken. Beavers continued to build dams and in some cases flood spruce swamps.

Timber was threatened, so the timber lobbyists went to work. The beaver trapping season was extended to include the spring, when trapping is easy. When the trapped mothers failed to return, the newborn young died, and the dams fell into disrepair. The ponds drained.

It was only when the fly fishermen complained loudly and effectively that beaver trapping was curtailed on a few creeks for a short distance inland from the North Shore.

On the Canadian side of the border trappers now take only one beaver from most of their houses each year. By careful trapping they can avoid catching the mother so as to assure themselves a sustained yield. They are not armchair conservationists, but conservationists in fact.

TRAPPING ON THE CANADIAN SIDE. Tempest Benson was raised on Saganagons Lake in the Jack Powell family of five children. Her parents gave the children a deep knowledge of animal habits as well as the ability and the confidence to live comfortably in the woods.

Each child was also given the basic elements of an educa-
tion and was taught to be self-sustaining and independent.
Tempest later shared this knowledge with her husband, Irv
Benson, who had returned to the North Country after serving
in World War II.

From time to time in 1961 Irv sent a newsletter, *Backtrail*,
to their friends and guests of their Pine Island Camp on
Saganaga Lake, Ontario. It provided fascinating descriptions
of his daily activities on his trap line. The following is quoted
from the *Backtrail* letter of December 4, 1961:

> Greetings from Saganagons Lake. During the past
> month much has taken place. The mice have been
> evicted from an otherwise empty cabin, and the logs
> have been chinked with new moss. Now each morn-
> ing and evening finds a column of smoke rising from
> the stovepipe. Though this location is only a matter
> of four or five miles from our home on the island in
> Saganaga, it's seemingly a different world altogether.
>
> I left from Saganaga on November 10th. Art Mad-
> sen brought me down to Silver Falls portage in Cache
> Bay with the boat and after a welcome assist across
> the trail I started down Saganagons in the canoe with
> an unlikely assortment of gear ranging from three
> sled dogs and a toboggan to a packsack loaded with
> sundry items, several cartons of eggs and a
> typewriter in a cardboard box. A steady southeast
> wind helped the 3-horse motor push the canoe along,
> and the east end of the lake was reached at 2 p.m. The
> winter supplies were already there, having been
> brought in by air the previous week." [Since this
> newsletter was written, planes have been banned
> from landing on Saganagons. Winter supplies now
> have to be packed over portages.]
>
> Monday, Nov. 13th: A most productive day. Caught

one large beaver on island near cabin and one mink on island near south shore midway down lake. Found another mink in trap at Moose Bay and set additional beaver and mink traps there. One mink and one muskrat in traps along Quetico Park line boundary, and found another mink in a trap on north shore that a raven had just started to eat—damaged slightly.

The evening was spent in skinning out the fur, the dogs welcoming their first feed of beaver meat since last spring. All the carcass went to them with the exception of the liver, which was my own supper.

The value of the beaver does not end with the pelt. Beaver is one of the main sources of fresh meat while on the trapline, tasting much like roast duck. The liver is as good or better than the best beef liver, and the heart and kidneys are also edible. The tail, which consists of fatty gristle covered by a scaly sheath, is edible or can be diced up and the fatty oil rendered out in a frying pan and used for leather boot water-proofing. Though trapping automatically brings first thoughts of mink, the beaver ranks highest when it comes to making use of the entire animal.

Along with these values the beaver is responsible for the creation of ponds behind his dams that pre-vent complete runoff of water. He also maintains reservoirs of water all along the creeks and rivers where he establishes residence. These in turn provide refuge and breeding areas for muskrat, mink, ducks and other waterfowl; and the water-lily filled ponds offer feeding areas for deer and moose.

Friday, Nov. 17th: [Irv had met Tempest at an open water portage and together they traveled to Bemar Lake where they checked traps.] During our walk back (on Bemar Lake where the newly formed ice was clear, smooth and two to three inches thick), Tempest told me how she'd seen her grandmother travel on smooth glare ice of newly frozen lakes. She would cut a block of ice eighteen inches wide and three feet long, bevel the front lower edge like a sled, put a folded packsack on the cake to sit on and push herself along the newly frozen lake by means of two sticks with nails driven into the lower ends. Upon coming to a portage, the sticks, or at least the nails, were retained, and a new block of ice cut out on the next lake.

Sunday, Nov. 26th: Art Madsen dropped in for a surprise visit while on a hunting trip, and it was nice to have company again. I offered this character a 'hot toddy' made of duplicating fluid and canned milk, but he refused. He doesn't respond to Saganagons hospitality at all.

Thursday, Nov. 30th: To date all of this traveling has been done on foot to be certain of good ice ahead, but as the east end of this lake, Bemar and Elevation Lake had a good ice cover I decided to begin breaking the dogs in for the winter. My lead dog has been sick this summer, but though he's still on the thin side, the recent meals of beaver meat have helped to put on a little of the weight he has lost. He still doesn't care much for my version of boiled fish and cornmeal dog food. Possibly my cooking is at fault, but I hesitate to taste the mixture to find out. The other two dogs eat it, but of course, there's little they won't eat. My definition of a sled dog is a big appetite with a mouth on one end and a tail on the other.

I put all three in harness this morning and made a circuit of Bemar and Elevation Lakes plus the portion of this end of Saganagons that is frozen, finding a beaver, a mink and a weasel in the traps previously set. The dogs seemed quite happy to get off their chains and back to work. It's amazing the way they can remember from last year where each trap is set and stop there without being told.

While I'm working at a trap they either watch or doze off a bit, but the moment I tie up the packsack and pick up the rifle they're on their feet and ready to go without a word being said. I rather think they know what's going on, as when I approach a trap, they watch closely until they see nothing has been caught. If something is in the trap, they usually smell it long before I reach the spot, and they are quite anxious to get up to see what's been caught. By watching the dogs continually testing the air as they travel along, one almost knows when something is nearby, be it deer, moose, any fur animal or what have you.

At the cabins on the trapline where the dogs have their bed of boughs at night instead of a doghouse, one can listen to the rattle of their chains on a snowy night as they shake off the newly fallen snow. One can tell by the interval between 'shakes' how hard the snow is coming down without getting up to look.

Curled into a ball of hair on their bough beds at night, they're warm in most any weather above or below zero. As I write this the dog chained to his house in the back of the cabin had just dragged his chain in and out of his abode for perhaps the fifteenth time tonight, sounding for all the world like Jacob Marley paying his nocturnal visit to Mr. Scrooge.

Though we have a gasoline-powered snow toboggan that can take us farther during the course of a day than the dog team, the dogs still remain the best form of transportation when it comes to travel on most parts of the trapline. They do not need a cut-out trail ahead of them, can haul a toboggan through any kind of a tangle one can snowshoe through, and with dogs, one never encounters mechanical difficulties.

Shortly after midnight tonight I was awakened by a
tremendous roaring of the lake ice. It has been creaking
and groaning during the early evening, and evidently
the forces of expansion and contraction from the freezing had all concentrated in one spot to form an
upheaval. At times these heaves, or pressure ridges,
pile up ice to a height of six feet and over, creating a
dangerous situation. Any disturbance to the piled up
blocks—such as trying to cross the ridge—can cause the
loosely piled ice to tumble back into the open water
beneath. Sometimes the heave is downward, rather
than above the lake ice surface. After a snowstorm, or
when the down heave is covered with snow, the fault
is a natural trap for any unwary person or animal
running into it and the open water underneath.

During the early part of the freeze-up period when
the ice is unprotected by the deep snow of later
winter, temperatures of zero and below cause the ice
to expand as it freezes. Hollow booming and crashing
and growling accompanies this expanding, contract-
ing and cracking ice, filling the night with sound—so
different from the dead still, dark hours of late winter.

Mailing date of this issue of the *Backtrail* will be
whenever the thermometer drops a few degrees and
adds a few inches of ice over on Saganaga to enable
Tempest, my 'mailman,' after carefully testing the ice,
to travel as far as the portage. Right now it's high time
to trade in the typewriter for the frying pan and
otherwise do justice to another fried beaver liver.

THOUGHTS. Times and values change, and we acquire new
perspectives with the passing of years. Hunting, during the
season, was in order in 1930 when people needed meat for
winter. Later when roads were improved and isolation was
no longer a factor meats, fruits and fresh vegetables were

easily attainable. At that time watching birds and animals in their natural habitat became much more appealing to me than killing them.

Sport hunting seems such a futile waste. It is so often carried out for the sake of gathering a pair of antlers or displaying a mounted head. In many instances the meat is left to spoil and rot.

The first fall, in 1927 when I came to Gunflint, I, accompanied by a guide, shot a moose. At that time my activities could easily have been considered sport hunting. There was one difference. Like the Indians, I helped to pack out and use every smidgen of the animal. There are still those who shoot deer for meat and waste nothing. There are fathers and mothers who take their sons or daughters into the woods to teach them the skill of hunting.

It should also be pointed out that I still enjoy deer or moose roasts. I have also found bear and beaver meat very tasty.

But this time in my life I find it more exciting to watch a partridge drum on a log and court its mate, to observe the development of the moose's antlers from the velvet stage to the final palmated spread. It is exciting to watch a deer guiding its spotted fawn through the woods or a tiny bear cub go tumbling after its mother. It is satisfying to see and hear the flocks of geese on their yearly flights.

These are my thoughts as this winter settles in.

DECEMBER

Solid Ice

WINTER SLOWLY INCHES ALONG. As cold air from the north meets the warmer air hanging over our lake, the lake becomes a cauldron of steam. The relentless north wind blows that steam across the lake and now has turned the entire south shore of the lake, and a stretch inland for a thousand feet, into a veritable hoarfrost fairyland. Each twig, tree, bush and protruding bit of moss is laden with masses of snow crystals. The trees, like tightly corsetted ladies, rustle their limbs as if encased in heavily starched skirts. The full moon at night creates shimmering shadows.

Like a youngster sneaking onto your porch to play a Halloween trick when no one is looking, winter slips in under cover of night and stealthily leaves a glaze of ice that covers the lakes.

On the Gunflint Trail the smaller lakes freeze over in November, and the larger, deeper lakes in mid-December. After the first glazing of ice, it takes five days of cold weather with no snow before you can be assured of reasonably safe travel.

However we still have to know our lakes. Where there is a spring, there may be a weak spot. Where there is a current, at the narrows between islands or lakes, there might be a skim of ice or no ice at all. Around a live beaver house or dam or near a rapids, the ice is often precarious.

When the lake first freezes over and a snowstorm follows, the snow acts as a blanket and slows the ice-thickening process. The heavy deposit of snow will, through its weight, cause the ice to sink. Where cracks have formed the water will ooze up under the blanket of snow. These spots become the slushy quagmires that you encounter in lake travel.

Ice has other idiosyncrasies too. When the air temperature rises from 14 to 32 degrees on a lake that is one mile across, the ice sheet will contract laterally approximately 32 inches. Ice is much stronger in compression than it is in expansion. So if the temperature drops again, trouble starts. The ice sheet tries to expand back to its original shape. The ice literally ruptures itself by forming cracks. Some cracks can be wide and others hairline.

The cracks don't remain open to allow room for the next expansion of the ice sheet. Instead, the water in the cracks

SOLID ICE

freezes, forming new ice and stealing the space that otherwise would have served to accommodate expansion.

As this expansion recurs upheavals of ice may develop
that extend upwards of three to six feet. On one side of this
ice ridge the ice may be weak.

For those who would venture forth onto our December
lakes, it's wise to learn the ways of ice.

TESTING ICE THE INDIAN WAY.   It has been a long time coming, but Irv Benson finally gave me a detailed account of
testing newly formed ice. It has been dubbed the "Saganaga
Shuffle" and has been used by Tempest Powell Benson and
her parents and grandparents. She has passed this informa-
tion on to her husband, Irv, who has passed it on to me.
According to Irv:

> One can't possibly go wrong on new ice with a
> trying pole, as long as the ice is not covered by so
> much snow as to muffle the sound of each tap or
> absorb the feel through the feet. Usually one can
> safely (according to one's weight, day temperature
> and type of ice) walk on two inches of new black ice.
> First cut a six- or seven-foot pole an inch and a half
> wide at the bottom end and an inch at the top end.
> Ends must be cut off square, not pointed. The idea is
> to thump the ice to get a tone rather than to try to poke
> a hole through the ice. The pole must be straight, as
> a bent one will not deliver the full force to the ice and
> will also tire the hand from vibration. In use, if one is
> right-handed, the pole is dropped about two inches
> away alongside the right foot, just as this foot is
> placed ahead for the next step.
> The initial dropping of the end of the pole onto the
> ice surface produces a thump with a certain tone.
> Thin ice has a high pitched ring. The tone deadens as

175

the ice gets thicker. Thick ice sounds like dropping the end of the pole on a concrete sidewalk. If the ice is quite thin, one feels a vibration through the ball of the right foot where the end of the pole thumped the ice alongside it. This gives you a secondary warning of thin ice along with the tone of the dropping.

One can visualize oil drums standing side by side with varying degrees of fullness—from empty to quarter-full to half-full to three-quarters to full. When tapped, each one will produce a different tone—just as long strings inside a piano produce a deeper tone than short ones when a mallet strikes them. This same principle is one hundred percent foolproof in indicating ice thickness, as long as one tests the ice correctly: you must drop the pole alongside the foot at every step, and when the tone changes to a higher pitch or more vibration is felt through the foot, you must stop to tap around in a semi-circular area ahead.

Your pole should be a good straight green ash or birch pole. As it strikes the ice, the upper end is a scant foot away from the right ear and the pole acts exactly like a tuning fork. A dry pole tends to ring of its own accord. This is not satisfactory for testing ice, as one wants to hear the tone of the ice, not the pole.

Now in case one does make a mistake (which is almost impossible if testing is done correctly and the individual has enough common sense to know when to back up), hold tightly to the pole and quickly switch it to a horizontal position to prevent you from going through the ice completely—or it can be used to climb out on the ice after the fact. A dry pole would simply snap in two, whereas a green one will bend or at the very most splinter but still remain intact.

Anytime one is traveling new ice and a definite step down is noticed ahead or felt with the foot (of approximately a quarter- to a half-inch lower) this means that the lower ice is newer by at least one night's freeze. This ice should be sounded out with a pole before venturing out on it. Earlier ice always floats up higher than surrounding open water, so a new freeze against older ice will always be at a lower level—sometimes as much as one inch.

Cold, dry snow on a thin layer of ice is pure poison for anything but sitting in. So is new glare ice glistening with a thaw as the sun is warming it. Even grease can't be more slippery.

Even if you've never been on the lake before, you do not need to be apprehensive about venturing onto newly formed ice, day or night. Just remember and use this way of testing ice just as Tempest, her family and their ancestors have done for generations in the past.

RAILROAD TREKS. The Port Arthur, Duluth and Western Railroad (later known as Poverty, Want and Distress) ran about 60 miles from Port Arthur to the Paulson Mine west of Gunflint Lake. It flourished in the 1890s and was abandoned in 1914. It remained somewhat intact until 1963, when the rail bed was covered, obliterating the past.

A portion of the modern-day Canadian highway from Whitefish Lake to Addie Lake was built alongside of or superimposed on the old railroad bed. The highway passes familiar names of old railroad stops: Mackies Siding, Round Lake, Sandstone, Iron Range, Prelate Lake and North Lake.

The old North Lake depot stood at the far eastern end of North Lake, complete with a bunker of coal. Through the two-story building passed potatoes, rutabagas, dog teams, toboggans and packsacks. The railroad also carried passengers from our border country to the wild rice fields of Whitefish Lake and to the fur buyers in the Canadian cities.

Although built to connect with the Paulson Mine, the railway also was used extensively in logging operations. Camp remnants are still found at Sac Bay on North Lake, at the North-South Lake Portage and at the east end of Gunflint Lake.

Great activity was centered on the Bishop homestead at the east end of North Lake, where at one time there was a large fox farm, an extensive garden, logging and fur buying. The railroad extended along the north shore of North Lake, crossing a far-reaching bay and trestle, now known as Burnt Trestle Bay, and continuing on to Gunflint Lake.

A spur took off at the mouth of Little Gunflint Lake, where Customs houses were located, crossed the 10-foot span of water to the Minnesota side and continued along the east shore of Gunflint to Crab Lake. An occasional piece of rail, switch, lever or rail spike still marks the way.

To reach the top of the ridge beside the thinly spread falls that spill over a cliff and are fed by waters from Crab Lake, a gravel fill was built. When the chasm became too great it was laboriously filled with logs, corduroyed tier after tier, and topped with gravel.

This old railroad bed was constructed before the era of mechanized power tools. It is a tribute to the accomplishments that can be attained with determination and simple tools: an ax, broad ax and adze. Most of this area was logged for its white pine and Norway pine and is crisscrossed by old logging roads and old railroad spurs.

Back at Little Gunflint, the main line extended along the north shore of Gunflint Lake to Le Blaine, where there are the remains of cabins built for the railroad workers.

Along this area are several rock ovens. A few are well preserved, while others have trees growing through the center. The ovens are built of rock in the shape of an igloo with a single front opening. A fire was built in the rock cavern. When the rocks were sufficiently heated, the coals were scraped out, bread shoved in and the door plugged. It was a most effective baking device.

The railway spanned the narrows between Gunflint Lake and Magnetic Bay by a high viaduct and followed the valley along the Cross River to the point now taken over by the Gunflint Trail. It extended onto what is now the Tuscarora Lodge road, where you can still pick up the right-of-way as well as a turnaround spur as it skirts along a hillside.

ON THE SKIDS.   It is rare in midwinter to have temperatures suddenly soar to 32 degrees, but it did happen to us in 1966. As a result for almost a week the Trail was on the skids—a condition we're more likely to face in March.

The weather turned warm, hovering between the above- and below-freezing marks. Tree branches that had carried their snow cover for weeks relaxed and hung limp. Great gobs of snow fell with a plop and rolled down the inclines to the road, leaving what appeared to be a row of beheaded snowmen along the shoulders.

When a misty fog descended the moisture was converted into ice as it lay on the pavement or gravel and it built up into a glassy smooth cover, inch by inch. This was before the County Highway Department sanded the hills. The glaze made the road impossible to walk or drive on with any degree of certainty.

Under these circumstances three of us in different cars and at different intervals started up the Trail. Eleanor Matsis, driving home from her teaching position in the Grand Marais school, was the first. Before she came to the Brule River she encountered the school bus with Pat McDonnell, the driver. The bus had slithered to the side of the road at the base of the hill and could make no further progress.

When Mat came upon the scene, she loaded the dozen youngsters in her station wagon and went on. Rolling over the top of the Bearskin hill, the front wheels of the station wagon failed to respond. A slow skid ensued as the car plowed into the snowbank.

I came along next, first reaching Pat. I stopped to talk. He elected to stay with the school bus, like a captain riding out a storm with his ship.

When I came upon Mat who was shoveling out her car, she suggested I take the youngsters on in my station wagon. As one wee one climbed aboard and looked me over with a critical eye, she remarked, "Well, this is the third one—will this last?"

A portion of the load disembarked at the Clearwater Road where there was a car waiting, and the balance were dropped off at the Hungry Jack Road where they started their after-dark, three-mile hike home.

At Trail Service Center Floyd Soderberg was comfortably relaxing before his TV but quickly reached for his boots when he learned that his help might be needed to go back and extricate a car. Mothers were called to assure them of their children's safety.

With Bette McDonnell the conversation went something like this: "Bette, the school bus is stuck, but the youngsters are all right and are walking in."

"Where's Pat?" she asked.

"He stayed with the school bus," I answered.

"What's he waiting for—Christmas?" she retorted.

While my car was being fitted with chains, Mat arrived after Jim Johnson and Carl Mort helped Bette get chains on her car. Russell Blankenburg had picked up Pat and had already been in and out of the ditch once. As we proceeded like a small caravan, Russell and Eve in their Jeep, and Mat and I in our respective station wagons, one car or another would slowly spin on a downhill slope and land against a snowbank.

As the occupants in each vehicle in turn stopped to help the others, the road became increasingly so slippery and treacherous on foot that we often had to crawl from one spot to the other on hands and knees.

At one point Russell attempted to use a shovel for support as he walked across the road. It was to no avail. As he slid down the hill, his voice became more distant. The receding words floated out of the darkness, "This is reminiscent of the old days when we had to help one another get anywhere."

In the wee hours of the morning the struggle was abandoned. The next day Eve and Russell returned to their vehicle with a pair of truck chains. They had caught a ride back down the Trail with Don Brazell in his mail car. Don was the master Trail driver, but even he had to use chains.

The chains didn't fit, so Eve came hiking into Gunflint Lodge with one long dark chain draped over her shoulder like a flowing scarf. Russell arrived five minutes later with the other chain tucked neatly in a small pack on his back.

Some time later, George Plummer came in and remarked, "I've never seen it so bad. It took me three hours to get here from Trail Center."

I replied, "Think nothing of it. Russell and Eve started here yesterday, and they aren't home yet."

MY HOME ON THE GUNFLINT.   After writing about trapping cabins one day I started to look at my own winter home.

Like the trapping cabins, this place, too, is a log cabin except for the addition of bedrooms and the large kitchen that was necessary for a growing family.

As I write it is winter. As happens in this season things are moved in. In a corner of the living room is a mini-chain saw with a can of oil. Another corner harbors several pair of snowshoes, a couple of canoe paddles, a fox stretcher handed down from some trapper, a pair of cross-country skis and boots, a pair of downhill skis (one is broken and is only a half ski), a packsack stuffed with a sleeping bag, a set of nesting pails, several fishing rods, a pair of hip boots for fly fishing and an assortment of parkas, boots, and a snowmobile suit hanging from one of the sundry nails. Otter and marten hides grace one log panel.

Of course there is a fireplace, shelves loaded with books, a TV, radio, camera equipment and electric lights. I have threatened to hoe the place out, but then how would I find what I was in looking for in the middle of the winter?

For me, this time of year is entwined with snowshoes, parkas, mukluks, woolen shirts, long johns, caps and mitts. In my car I always include, as standard equipment, a snow shovel, ax and matches.

When I am clad in "store-bought clothes," I have ample winter togs packed in a box in the car trunk to assure a margin of safety in case of need.

Few of these items would be necessary for city dwellers. But in these Northwoods in the winter where traffic is often light and miles separate any occupied dwellings, attention to safety is of critical importance.

In 1987 I was swept up in the change that has become part of life on the Trail when my son Bruce updated and modernized my home. Sagging parts of the old building were torn out and rebuilt.

Now I have a log cabin with a computer, new spacious windows, a modern bathroom and bedroom, and a kitchen complete with a dishwasher. Added to this bonanza is a garage, a heated workshop and a satellite dish that provides perfect TV reception.

This only partially illustrates the numerous changes that have affected the homes and resorts along the Gunflint Trail. The conversion has come gradually over a period of years as we've gone from individual light generators, outside toilets, gasoline lanterns, no running water and a grounded-circuit, single-wire telephone line that worked erratically at best, to the present ultramodern accommodations.

Time on the Trail.   Along the Gunflint Trail time is marked by weather and events rather than by months, weeks, days or hours. Conventional units for measuring time have a way of losing their identity. On the Gunflint nature sets its own calendar.

Even the years would blend into each other except for the memorable events that set one apart from another. If you were to ask our Indian neighbors when they were born, they would say "the year of the deep snow" or "the year of the fires" or "the year the trees blew down."

Irv Benson once observed, "If folks would only quit looking at the calendar and leave their wristwatches at home, they could keep those little crevices of their brain open to take in some of the more interesting things that are all over the place here on the Trail."

In my sixty-plus years on the Trail I have lived through many snows, fires and storms—and the many changes imposed on this area by humans. Often I've followed Irv's advice and left my wristwatch at home. I've done what the weather would let me do, or what the seasons encouraged me to do—not what the calendar said it was time for. Over the years the little crevices in my brain have been opened to countless happenings and events, large and small, happy and sad.

Reflections.   We know, though seldom remember in our self-centered living, that from the distance of the heavens humans seem non-existent and the earth itself appears as no more than a globe of reflected light, spinning from day to night, an infinitesimal speck in an ever-expanding universe.

North Country Christmas

In the cathedral of the north,
a million stars dot the heavens
flickering like candles
held by the people of the universe
in a moment of peace and reverence.

The pines are cloaked in mantles of white
as they sway in gentle harmony
with the symphony of the sighing wind.

A padded footstep crunching faintly on the crisp snow
is accompanied by a furtive shadow
that quickly vanishes,
for the moonlight has turned the night
into a world of half tones and dancing reflections
from the carefully formed snow crystals
that cling tenaciously to every branch and twig.

The restless lake, quieted and confined,
now serves as a carpet
on which otter caper, wolves roam
and deer tred capriciously.

It is here where solitude is eminent
and living needs are simple and uncluttered

that there is time to hesitate
and reevaluate the hodgepodge of life.

It is here too that gifts are exchanged
perhaps more from necessity than virtue
in the form of needed understanding
a kindness
or unsolicited help.

The weaving and intermittent colored lights
playing across the northern horizon
are accentuated by an occasional falling star.

With the coming of dawn
the wonders of the night fade and vanish
and there is an interim
when all sounds seem to cease.

As we attend this sunrise service
the heavens bring forth a rosy glow
that fills our hearts
with new hope and refreshed ideas.

So again the forest becomes alive
to accept the challenge of a new day.
                                    [Christmas 1970]

Epilogue

 # Epilogue

THE LANDS AND WATERS of our community that are dear to my heart have been subjected to fluctuating and inconsistent management philosophies for many years.

Over time the values, perspectives and priorities of the people who are interested in and use the Boundary Waters Canoe Area have changed. Many of these changes have led to legislation and management policies that have created controversy and hardship.

The wilderness continues to be buffeted by special-interest groups more invested in demanding that their agendas be adopted than in looking at the big picture of effects on the environment. All the involved parties like to be considered environmentalists. It is a challenging task to figure out when they become extremists with demands that are out of focus for the good of the resource.

Just when things seem to be falling into place, there are new clouds on the horizon. The current management rules seem sufficient and appropriate to the resources, and recreational visitors have accepted and adjusted to these rules. However there are still some groups who will not leave the rules alone. Every few years the Boundary Waters Area seems to become a management battleground—political management, not resource management.

Some people want more lands and waters restricted for paddle canoeists only. Some want fewer users, while others would like to lock up the area as a primitive scientific area in a world biosphere, visited only by scientists from around the world. Usually people mess up most of what they try to manage in nature.

But through all the mishmash yet to come, I trust Mother Nature will prevail, and our Boundary Waters Wilderness will continue to be the special area I have been fortunate enough to have lived in for most of my life.